SECONDARY WORLDS

W. H. AUDEN

SECONDARY WORLDS

*The T. S. Eliot Memorial Lectures
Delivered at Eliot College
in the University of Kent at Canterbury,
October 1967*

faber and faber
LONDON · BOSTON

First published in 1968
by Faber and Faber Limited
3 Queen Square London WC1N 3AU
This edition first published in 1984
Filmset by Goodfellow & Egan Limited
Printed in Great Britain by
Whitstable Litho Limited
Whitstable, Kent

British Library Cataloguing in Publication Data

Auden, W. H.
Secondary worlds
1. Literature – History and criticism
I. Title
809 PN523
ISBN 0-571-13221-9

For
VALERIE ELIOT

CONTENTS

FOREWORD

As the person who has the signal honour and grave responsibility of inaugurating these lectures founded in memory of T. S. Eliot, it seemed to me that the first question I should ask myself was: upon what themes, if he were in a position to give his opinion, would Mr Eliot like them to be? My only certainty was negative: given his character as a man, and the contemporary critical scene, he would *not* wish me to devote them to his own work. In his own lifetime, interpretation and evaluations of his writings had assumed the proportions of a heavy industry, and I know that this both amused and dismayed him. It seemed to me that what he would most probably wish would be some further discussion of questions which were close to his heart, as a poet, a dramatist, and a twentieth-century Christian.

For anyone familiar with his critical writings, it is not difficult to draw up a list of these. But it was not easy for me – nor, I think, would it be for anyone else – to select from my list topics about which I could feel I had the competence, or at least the nerve, to speak.

In this my first lecture, its relation to Eliot's interests is pretty direct. The hero of his first full-length play was a historical martyr, Becket; Harry, the hero of *Family Reunion*, though we are not told what happens to him, decides to take up a way of life which may well lead – as a similar decision by Celia, the heroine of *The Cocktail Party*, actually does – to martyrdom.

11

In my other three, the relation is less direct and may seem to some nonexistent. Eliot never, to my knowledge, wrote about the Icelandic sagas and, indeed, I do not know if he ever read them. I was brought up on them as a child, and they have remained ever since among my favourite works of literature, so it could be sheer selfishness on my part to drag them in. I hope and believe, though, that this is not the case. The relation between those secondary worlds which we call works of art and the primary world of our everyday social experience is a problem which concerns every artist, and the successful 'social' realism of the sagas has its peculiar light to throw on this general problem.

Eliot never wrote about music and, much to my regret, never wrote an opera libretto, but from the verse play, in which he took a life-long interest, to the opera libretto is a short step.

Mr Eliot was a poet writing in English in the twentieth century; he was also a Christian. Nobody can be both without asking himself two questions: 'What difference, if any, do my beliefs make, either to what I write, or to my conception of my vocation? Secondly, in what ways do the problems of a Christian writing in this century differ from those of a Christian writing in earlier periods?' To these I shall devote my last lecture.

I

THE MARTYR AS DRAMATIC HERO

In myth, history and literature, we meet four kinds of human being, of whom it may be said that their deaths are the most significant event in their lives, the Sacrificial Victim, the Epic Hero, the Tragic Hero and the Martyr.

THE SACRIFICIAL VICTIM

In societies that offer human sacrifices, a man is chosen by a social group to die to promote its spiritual and material welfare; his blood must be shed in order that crops may grow or the wrath of the gods be appeased. However the victim be selected, whether he be the consort of the mother-priestess or a prisoner of war, and whether he consents to his death or not, his role is decided by others, not by himself. In some cultures, in the interval between his being designated as a sacrificial victim and the act of sacrifice itself, he is treated as a sacred person to whom honour is paid and special licence given, but once he has been sacrificed his role is over and he is forgotten.

THE EPIC HERO

Like the sacrificial victim, the Epic Hero dies for the sake of a social group; he falls while battling against its enemies. But in his case, it is not the social group that chooses him. He becomes a hero, partly by fate – he is born with exceptional qualities of strength and courage – and partly by his own choice. Secondly, though it is usually his fate to fall in battle, death is not his goal; his goal is to slay the enemies of his people and by his valiant deeds to win immortal glory, to be remembered by generation after generation.

THE TRAGIC HERO

The Tragic Hero is an individual who in some way or other becomes guilty – either, like Oedipus, in the eyes of the gods or, like Macbeth, in the eyes of men. He suffers and dies not for the sake of others but as a punishment and in expiation of his guilt. His story is remembered by others precisely because it is an exceptional and spectacular fall from fortune to disaster, glory to misery, which could not happen to the average audience. The chorus are not in any way involved with his fate: they are pure spectators.

THE MARTYR

The Martyr is a sacrificial victim, but in his case it is he who chooses to be sacrificed, or rather – and in this he resembles the Epic Hero – it is his destiny to be sacrificed and he accepts his destiny. Those for whose sake he sacrifices himself do not choose him as an atoning sacrifice; on the contrary, they deny that any sacrifice has been made. To them he is a criminal, blasphemer, disturber of the social order, and though, like that of the Epic Hero, his death is a spectacle, it is not for the spectators a tragic or a sacred but a profane event, the execution of a common criminal. The Martyr sacrifices himself not for the sake of any particular individual or social group but for all mankind. In the special case of Christ, the God-Man, he dies to redeem sinful mankind; the ordinary human martyr dies to bear witness to what he believes to be saving truth, to be shared by all men, not reserved as an esoteric secret for a few. The conception of saving truth is a highly dangerous one, for those who believe that it can be a duty to die for the truth can come all too easily to believe that it is also a

14

duty to kill for it. The history of the Christian Church – no other religious body has killed so many people for doctrinal reasons – has taught us that we cannot reserve the title of martyr for those who die for beliefs that coincide with our own, that a man who dies to bear witness to dialectical materialism is no less a martyr than one who dies to bear witness to the Nicene formulae. One can say, however, that it was Christianity and the cultures influenced by it that first recognized the Martyr as a classifiable type. All the so-called higher religions regard one person as their founder and head, but only in the case of Christianity did this person suffer a violent and degrading death. If the world now knows that at all times in history and in all places there have been martyrs, it is largely Christianity which is responsible. I would go further and say that if any man, whatever his beliefs, were told the story of two martyrs and asked to say which was the noblest or purest example of martyrdom, his standard of comparison would be based, consciously or unconsciously, upon the story of the Crucifixion.

He would say, for example, that, for martyrdom in its purest form, one condition is that the Martyr dies absolutely alone and forsaken, surrounded only by official executioners, enemies and sadistic or idly curious spectators. So it was with Christ. The Fourth Gospel records that Mary, his mother, Mary Magdalene and John, his closest friends as human beings, stood by his Cross during his Crucifixion, but they stood there, surely, out of loyal affection to the Manhood, not in recognition of his Godhead. And before the end he must endure not only desertion by men but the withdrawal of His Father's presence, total isolation.

A second condition is that the Martyr's death must be one of extreme agony and physical humiliation in which all self-respect is lost. As Charles Williams has written: 'Our crucifixes exhibit the pain, but they veil, perhaps necessarily, the obscenity: but the death of the God-Man was both.'

Last, to those who witness his death he must seem to have died to no purpose. Nothing happens to vindicate, beyond all doubt, the cause for which he has died. Christ did not convert the whole world in an instant by appearing in glory on the First Easter Sunday. He appeared in private to his disciples and entrusted them with the task of converting the world; they were to preach to the world that He had risen from the dead, an event for which they could offer no proof.

In the light of these remarks, let us examine briefly two accounts of pre-Christian martyrs, the story of Antigone as told by Sophocles and the story of Socrates as told in the *Phaedo*. Antigone's two brothers, Eteocles and Polynices, have both fallen in battle, Eteocles in defence of the city of Thebes, Polynices in an attempt to invade and destroy it. In all societies the traitor is regarded with abhorrence, so that Creon's decree that Polynices' body shall be denied burial and funeral rights may be thought excessively vindictive but not self-evidently evil. Antigone, knowing that the penalty for disobeying the decree is death, nevertheless defies it, buries her brother, is caught and condemned to death. The cause for which she is prepared to die is a particular, not a universal, cause. She does not say – no Greek would – that in all circumstances loyalty to and affection for one's blood kin must take precedence over loyalty to one's city. If, for example, instead of getting killed Polynices had been taken prisoner, she would not, I think, have considered it unjust if Creon had put him to death. But in her view, the brother she loves has expiated his crime by death and has therefore the right to the burial rites which relatives pay to their dead. Moreover, in this view, she is not alone. The majority of the citizens of Thebes approve of her action. So does Creon's own son, who is engaged to her. Tiresias appears and prophesies terrible disasters. Creon at last relents and cancels the death sentence, but it is too late. His son and his wife have killed themselves. For Sophocles the

16

principal figure in the tragedy is not Antigone but Creon. The role of Antigone is to reveal the fact that Creon is, and probably always has been, guilty of *hubris*. The disaster which befalls him is not a punishment for his treatment of Antigone but a punishment for his *hubris* towards the gods of which his treatment of Antigone is a symptom. Had Antigone decided to obey his decree, then sooner or later some other train of events would have revealed his *hubris* and led to a similar punishment.

Socrates dies to bear witness to the Examined Life. Though this is a less particular cause than blood kinship, it is still far from being a universal. The Examined Life is for the select intelligent few, not for the uneducated or barbarian masses, who neither desire it nor are capable of practising it.

At his trial, as recounted in the *Apology*, Socrates treats his accusers with good-natured contempt as his inferiors. He claims to be a benefactor of Athens, who should be rewarded not punished. He discusses various alternatives to the death penalty. Imprisonment, exile, he says, would be certain evils, whereas he does not know enough about death to know whether it is a good or an evil. He suggests, therefore, a fine of thirty *minae*, which his friends will pay. Such words are clearly intended to insult. He is condemned to death, but the method of execution is singularly painless – many, probably most, deaths from natural causes are much more bitter. Moreover, he does not die in isolation but surrounded by his dearest friends and disciples, and the gradual and painless nature of his death allows him to go on discussing, very intelligently and at great length, philosophical problems. One of the nicest touches in the *Phaedo* is the incident with the executioner, who kindly warns him that he shouldn't talk so much as talk delays the action of the poison.

For both the humanist and the poet Socrates is the ideal martyr. The Crucifixion, on the other hand, can be neither humanized nor idealized. To attempt to poetize the dread-

17

ful facts is to falsify them. It is significant, I think, that the first piece of writing in mediaeval literature which can be called vulgar is the *Stabat Mater*.

It is not surprising that the predecessors of the humanists, Gnostics, refused to stomach the facts and preferred to believe that it was not Christ's real body that was crucified on the Cross but a phantasmal body, or the body of Judas Iscariot. The same natural aversion shows itself in many of the early hagiographies, where the martyrs are subjected to the most fantastic tortures without feeling any pain.

During the persecutions the Church discovered that there was an ethical-psychological problem about martyrdom which no one had foreseen, namely, that a man could get himself martyred not in order to bear witness to the truth on earth but in order to win for himself immortal glory in Heaven. In other words, his real motive could be the pride of the Epic Hero. The Church found herself having to preach caution and discourage her converts from insisting on martyrdom when it could possibly be avoided. Only when the choice lay between martyrdom and apostasy was martyrdom to be chosen. Here again, the story of the Passion is the paradigm. Far from rushing joyfully upon death, in the Garden of Gethsemane Christ prays in agony that the cup shall pass from him.

In 1935, for the Canterbury Festival, Eliot wrote *Murder in the Cathedral*; in the following year the festival play, written by his friend Charles Williams, was *Thomas Cranmer*. Though Becket and Cranmer were both prominent political figures, Eliot and Williams are less concerned with their secular historical significance than with their religious significance as martyrs. If I am going to devote most of this lecture to Williams's play, one reason is that *Murder in the Cathedral* has been read by everybody interested in modern poetry and frequently performed in many countries, while *Thomas Cranmer* has been read, I believe, by few, and seen by still fewer.

18

But I must begin by comparing the characters and circumstances of their respective heroes, for each presents the dramatist with a different problem. In neither case, as I said, is it a question of the cause for which they died. One may well think that Henry II was just in demanding that criminous clerks be tried in the King's courts or that Cranmer's views on the sacraments were heretical. That is not the point.

The question that worries me about Becket is whether his murder was not too accidental to warrant being called martyrdom. A little more than three hundred years later, when Sir Thomas More, who as Lord Chancellor was officially the Keeper of the King's Conscience, refused to acknowledge that Henry VIII was the Supreme Head of the English Church, he knew exactly what would happen to him. He would be tried for high treason, found guilty and executed. (Actually he was luckier than he expected, for he was only beheaded, not hung, drawn and quartered.) He knew that the Pope could do nothing to save him from death or to avenge it. He knew that, though there might be some of his fellow countrymen who agreed with him, none of them would dare protest.

But at the end of the twelfth century the situation was very different. The Pope was far stronger politically than Henry II. It would have been quite impossible for Henry to have Becket put to death by legal means. Becket had the backing of the Pope and, in addition, was very popular, apparently, with the common people. Henry was far too astute a politician not to know that if anything happened to Becket for which he could be held responsible, he would be in a very precarious position indeed, and that the first consequence would be that he would have to yield on all the points over which he and Becket were struggling. Unfortunately for him, he went into one of those famous Angevin rages, and the four knights acted on his inarticulate noises. The action of the four knights, incidentally, has always seemed to me the most mysterious event in the story, as they must have known that at times Henry was, to say the least, not quite himself. And how can they ever have imagined that, if they did kill Becket, it would be possible for Henry to reward them, even if he wanted to?

As Eliot makes the Third Knight say:

> ... *we* are not getting a penny out of this. We know perfectly well how things will turn out. King Henry – God bless him – will have to say, for reasons of state, that he never meant this to happen; and there is going to be an awful row; and at the best we shall have to spend the rest of our lives abroad.

From the point of view of a life insurance company, Becket had little to fear by returning to England. Eliot gets round this by letting Becket – with what historical justification I don't know, but dramatically it is perfectly legitimate and credible – have inner premonitions that to return to England will mean his death. Despite them he does return, and we cannot imagine him doing otherwise, for as a character Becket is the stuff of which epic heroes are made, utterly fearless, combative and very conscious of his natural *arête*. If he foresees his own death, he also, knowing the political circumstances and religious climate of the time, foresees what will follow: canonization, a splendid shrine, pilgrimages, a cult of veneration – in other words, glory on earth. He is pre-eminently one of those cases of martyrdom over which the question of motive – did he die for the truth or out of spiritual pride and ambition? – must arise. This is, from the religious point of view, the most crucial point; unfortunately, what his motive was cannot be dramatically manifested. Eliot shows Becket confronted successively by four tempters. The first three suggest various lines of conduct and policy, each of which would save his life. The Fourth Tempter urges him to get martyred in order to win posthumous glory in heaven and on earth. We hear him say no to all four. In the case of the first three we discover that he meant what he said, for we see him lose his life. In the case of the fourth all we know for certain is that he is aware of the temptation in himself: when the curtain falls we cannot know beyond all doubt whether he has really rejected or really yielded to it, since the manifest event we have witnessed, his death, would be the same in either case.

In Cranmer's case his character, his life, his recantation in order to escape the stake exclude the possibility of pride as a motive. The dramatic problem he presents is different. Had Becket died in his bed, he would now be remembered only by professional historians. Had Cranmer done the same, he would still be famous as the principal author of the Book of Common Prayer. He was, that is to say, both a man of action and an artist, a maker. A dramatist who takes him for his hero cannot ignore his making, for it is an essential aspect of his life and character, but it is impossible to represent convincingly on the stage a man writing a book, because of the time it takes. Williams shows Cranmer the maker by indirect illustration; from time to time he halts the action to let a choir sing appropriate passages from the Book of Common Prayer. This works for persons like myself who have been familiar with the words from childhood and know their source, but I fear that those who are less intimate with them may be irritated and feel that the choir is there only because this is a 'churchy' play.

The world of the eleventh century was a relatively stable world, united in doctrine and rite and taking its feudal social structure for granted. Eliot can therefore present the common people as a united chorus of spectators to events which they cannot influence. What they may have to suffer, injustice from their superiors, bad harvests, are part of the natural order of things, to be endured because they cannot be changed: tomorrow will be like today, neither better nor worse.

In speaking of its stability, I must emphasize the word 'relative'. Then, as in all periods, heresies or divergencies of belief existed, but in the twelfth century these involved only minorities. The Gregorian claim that the spiritual power had the right and duty to coerce the secular powers was certainly a revolutionary issue, but it concerned only those who, in this world, commanded real temporal power; whoever won, the powerless majority would have to obey.

The sixteenth century, on the other hand, was a period of fanatical doctrinal controversy – which, thanks to the invention of printing, involved the majority – and of revolutionary social change, so that no class and no individual could foretell what tomorrow might bring: to remain a purely passive spectator was almost impossible. Consequently, even had he wished to, it would have been very difficult for Williams to use a united chorus. Instead he uses the expressionistic device of type-figures, representative of the irreconcilable ideological and economic positions, who cannot argue with but only abuse each other, like the Catholic Priest and the Protestant Preacher:

THE PRIEST: The Lord remember you!

THE PREACHER: The Lord remember you!

THE PRIEST: Because you have forsaken him alone, the Lord shall smite you with scabs and emerods.

THE PREACHER: Because you have followed lying gods, the Lord shall set over you gods of stone.

THE PRIEST: Atheist!

THE PREACHER: Idolater!

THE PRIEST: Beast!

THE PREACHER: Devil!

Will you silence God's Word?

THE PRIEST: Will you touch God's altar?

You shall come to the fire with your hands in a halter.

THE PREACHER: And the Lord shall fling you to your own evil.

or like the two lords, who are agreed because they share the same secular interests. They profess moral indignation at the immorality of the monasteries, but it is, of course, in their interests that the charges of immorality should be true; the worse the monks are behaving, the better chance they have of acquiring their lands. To each other they are quite open about this.

1ST LORD: Sir, behold a formula – a device fitted,
2ND LORD: a confession due to the King of criminal follies;
1ST LORD: those that will sign – simple men misled.
2ND LORD: Sir, dissolve them graciously; take the land.
1ST LORD: Those that stand obstinately in sin, contending
2ND LORD: that they never did what we have written they
do –
1ST LORD: or that some do; if they deny that all do.
2ND LORD: Sir, dissolve them mightily; seize the gold.
BOTH: It were good the gentry of England had their goods.

In his treatment of time and space Eliot keeps as close as he can to the unities of Greek tragedy – the action takes place in a few critical days at the end of Becket's life with minimal changes of scene. Again, it is the relative stability of the eleventh century, I think, that makes this possible. One might say that there were only two significant events in Becket's life, his change of heart on becoming Archbishop from a King's to a Pope's man, and his death. Cranmer's life, both outer and inner (and this is the case with nearly all sixteenth-century figures) was continuously changing and unpredictable. To represent it adequately could not be done within the framework of the classical unities.

In Williams's play time and space are purely subjective, as they are in mediaeval mystery and miracle plays. On stage there are no time breaks and no changes of scenery; but it covers twenty-eight years of Cranmer's historical life, from 1528 to 1556, nineteen of them under Henry VIII, five under Edward VI and the two he spent in disgrace under Mary before he was finally executed. It must be admitted that, now and again, such compression must puzzle any audience that is not well acquainted with the historical facts. For instance, in hearing the following passage of dialogue:

2ND LORD: I have a plan for the Throne.
   The judges agree; the Council agrees; all men agree to the plan I have made. The King agrees. The King commands
                                                     you to agree.
CRANMER: I will see the King.
   It is my right: I will see the King alone.
2ND LORD: You shall not see the King more than I let you,
   nor alone, nor with any of your loyal, simple sort. The King commands you, on your allegiance, agree.
CRANMER: If the King commands –

there is nothing in the words themselves to tell the audience that the Second Lord's plan is that Lady Jane Grey, not Mary, should succeed to the throne, or that Cranmer's unfinished sentence means that he signed the act so devising the crown, the one deed in his life for which historians seem to be unanimous in condemning him.

Williams is primarily interested in Cranmer's inner life, his wishes, his motives and his moral choices, and with his public actions only in so far as they are manifestations of these.

How is a man's inner life to be made manifest on a stage? Not by dialogue, obviously, for when we speak to others we seldom, if ever, tell them all that is in our minds. Nor by soliloquies: we are never fully conscious of what we feel and are doing; ignorance of ourselves and self-deceptions are necessary to life, for complete consciousness would render us incapable of doing anything at all. Our inner life can be fully known only to God. Williams, therefore, introduces into his play, and assigns the principal role to, a divine agent he calls *Figura Rerum*, who can reveal to the audience what Cranmer cannot tell them of himself. I will return to this figure later. All I will say at this point is that, in my opinion, Williams succeeds in what I would have thought was impossible, namely, in creating a symbolic figure who is not an embarrassing bore. The Tempters in *Murder in the Cathedral* are symbolic figures, but they have short and minor parts; they are not put to the test of the star role.

In the sixteenth century all parties, Roman Catholic, Lutheran, Calvinist, were in agreement upon two points: (1) for their souls' sake and for the salvation of society, all men must believe in the True Faith; (2) all men will never be converted to the True Faith by argument and spiritual authority alone – uniformity of belief can be secured only if the temporal power, that is the Prince, imposes it.

We who have grown up in the twentieth century are perhaps in a better position to understand both presuppositions than those who lived in the past two centuries, when the presuppositions of the enlightenment and liberalism were taken for granted by all intelligent persons. On the issue of faith and works, for example, by liberal standards, the Roman Catholics of the sixteenth century, no less than their opponents, took the Protestant position, that is to say, they too held that faith is more important than works; a heretic might lead a better life than an orthodox worldly prelate, but he could not on that account be left alone. For the liberal the only standard is works, i.e., acceptable social behaviour; so long as a man behaves decently, it is nobody's business what he believes. In our own time we have seen this assumption challenged and a return to dogma, only in a political form. Again, the appearance in our time of dictatorships and one-party states has made it easier for us to understand what the doctrine of the Divine Right of Kings really meant. As C. S. Lewis has written:

It is best understood as the first form of something which has continued to affect our lives ever since – the modern

25

theory of sovereignty. Total freedom to make what laws it pleases, superiority to law because it is the source of law, is (now) the characteristic of every state, of democratic states no less than monarchical ... We take it for granted that the highest power in the state, whether that power is a despot, or a democratically elected assembly, will be wholly free to legislate and incessantly engaged in legislation.

In practice, to be sure, in democracies where there is more than one party the party in power will refrain from imposing certain legislation which its majority would allow it to do out of a prudent fear of losing the next election, but theoretically it can do whatever it likes.

The formulation and acceptance of the doctrine does not mean that in the sixteenth century kings acquired a sacral quality which they had previously lacked; on the contrary, it is a symptom that the archaic world, with its magic and sacral bonds, which had endured from pre-historic times, was beginning to collapse; the doctrine emerges precisely because rulers had lost their sacral aura; what it really attempts to do is to provide a theory to explain why a purely secular, i.e. profane, power must be obeyed. The boy *rois fainéants* of the Merovingians, though politically speaking they were puppets of the Mayor of the Palace, were held to be sacred beings in a way that Henry VIII never was.

Pope Gregory and his successors were the first to attempt to desacralize the archaic world. In place of the king and feudal lord, often a lord bishop, who was sacred by blood, they wished to substitute the Pope and his spiritual vassal, the celibate priest, made sacred by ordination. Initially they had some success, but the effect of Avignon and the great Schism was to weaken popular belief in their sacrality; the Divine Right of Kings and the Priesthood of all Believers are two sides of the same coin.

Shakespeare is misleading here because he was a poet and, like all poets, even today, his imagination was rooted in the archaic world view.

Williams's play opens in 1528, when Cranmer is 38 years old, already a widower, a priest for five years, a fellow of Jesus College, Cambridge and a happy man.

> Coming in from the gallop, I vault on language, halt
> often but speed sometimes, and always heed
> the blessed beauty of the shaped syllables. I would let go
> a heresy or so for love of a lordly style
> with charging challenge, or one that softens a mile
> to a furlong with dulcet harmony, enlarging
> the heart with delicate diction. Come,
> today's journey waits: open gates! Blessed Lord,
> thou hast given me horses, books, Cambridge, and peace:
> foolish the man, having these, who seeks increase.

Whatever or whomever we love carries with it a temptation to its own special kind of idolatry: those who, like Cranmer, love words are tempted to idolize them. Idolatry of the word can express itself, according to the temperament of the individual, either in a fanatic dogmatism which identifies language with truth or in an aestheticism which sets beauty of language above truth. For Cranmer, essentially a timid and gentle man, it was clearly not dogmatism but aestheticism that was the danger. Faced with the possibility of martyrdom, the dogmatist, certain that *he* is right, is tempted to insist upon dying for *his* truth; the aesthete, confronted with a reality where beautiful words are no help, is tempted to apostatize.

Without attempting to tell us exactly what Cranmer's theological position was at this time, Williams shows him as already disturbed by the late mediaeval emphasis on adoration of the consecrated host at the expense of communion:

> now are means of communion adored
> yet dyked from approach; untrod, unexplored,
> is the road; instead of God are God's marvels displayed,
> rivals to Christ are Christ's bounties made,
> and dumb are our people: negligent they lie and numb.
> Our Father, in whom is heaven, thy kingdom come.

As if in answer to his prayer, there now enters a non-human symbolic figure, *Figura Rerum*, the most important role in the play. As with all genuine symbolic creations, he is much easier to grasp imaginatively than to analyse, for analysis always tends to reduce symbolism to a false and boring allegory. However, I must try to say something. Dressed as a skeleton, he is at the simplest level, the traditional *Mors*. When Anne Boleyn is condemned to death, he covers her with his cloak and leads her out; when he touches the King, Henry says: 'Thomas, I am dying.'

But physical death is but a very small part of his significance. Though he often addresses those on stage as well as commenting on them to the audience, he is invisible to them, yet at certain moments of fear and crisis they respond as if aware of his presence, and in the case of Anne Boleyn and Cranmer their words and his sentences so correspond with each other as to sound like a dialogue. When, as Edward VI is dying, Cranmer first begins to realize what may be in store for him, *Figura Rerum* even becomes a visible presence to him but not as we, the audience, see him.

SKELETON: My lord!
CRANMER: Friend, do I know you?
    Are you of my household?
SKELETON: An indweller,
             my lord;
  a copier-out, a carrier-about
      . . . an errand-runner.
CRANMER: My eyes are weak; forgive me, if I should know
               you.

Here are a few things he says about himself:

We of heaven are compassionate-kind;
we give men all their mind;
asking, at once, before they seek, they find.

I am the delator of all things to their truth.

28

I am the Judas who betrays men to God.

I am Christ's back.

As a messenger and agent of God, he has certain affinities with the Satan of the Book of Job; he can read men's hearts; he understands their weaknesses and self-deceptions and is permitted to put them to tests which they may well fail; he represents, that is to say, that aspect of the divine activity we have in mind when, in the Lord's Prayer, we pray, 'Lead us not into temptation but deliver us from evil.' He is also, in a sense, the voice of the Holy Spirit, of the truth which forces upon our attention the reality which, as Eliot says, we cannot bear very much of: for that reason too, the silence of the void, the dark night of the soul, when everything in which we have trusted fails, the experience which, the Gospels tell us, even Christ had to endure.

To wish is always dangerous. Had Cranmer, the don, really wished for nothing but the horses, books, Cambridge and peace he had been granted, he might have ended his days as a quiet, selfishly happy scholar. But in fact he desires more than good for himself; he desires good for others as he sees it and looks to the King to bring them that good:

> O that the King, O that God's glory's gust
> from heaven would drive the dust of the land, smite
> his people with might of doctrine, embodied raise
> their subservient matter, set with his fire ablaze
> their heavy somnolence of heavenly desire, his word
> bid what God said be heard, what God bade be done!
> that the King's law might run savingly through the land:
> so might I, if God please, outcast from my brethren stand.

In wishing thus, Cranmer shows that he has as yet very little idea of what Henry is really like, either in character – a prince, certainly, but hardly a godly one – or in his theological opinions. To the end of his days Henry remained

a strictly orthodox Roman Catholic on all points of doctrine
except the supremacy of the Pope. While he lived, there
was no chance of Cranmer's conception of God's word
becoming the law of the land. But with this wish in his
heart chance, or providence, brings Cranmer and the
King together.

In July 1529 Henry was hunting at Waltham. His
chaplain, Fox, and his secretary, Gardiner, were staying
with the Cressys, where Cranmer was tutor. At table,
conversation turned upon the divorce from Catherine
which Henry was seeking. Cranmer suggested that the
quickest method would be to obtain the opinion of all the
great theological universities, at home and abroad. Fox
and Gardiner mentioned his remarks to the King. The
King liked the idea and summoned Cranmer. Four years
later, as a reward for his services, Cranmer was made
Archbishop of Canterbury. Charles Williams compresses
the whole of this period into two pages, climaxing in
Cranmer's decision to accept the archbishopric, about
which, in historical time, he took six months to make up
his mind.

THE KING: There must be an archbishop to beget me an heir
    legitimately and canonically.
    I am the head. Be Canterbury, Thomas.
    The Pope nods to me; he will send the pall . . .
    Be swift; determine the cause; pronounce this month
    the dispensation invalid, the marriage null.
    Terrible to the land is the trouble of the King.
CRANMER: I am no man for this; I am purblind,
    weak, for my courage was shouted out of me
    by schoolmasters and other certain men.
    thought is slow, uncertain of itself, willing to serve
    God and its friends and peace –
THE KING: The will of the King is as the will of God.
SKELETON: Besides, even your thought must consider your
                                       world . . .

    Even a shy man must make up his mind.

> Has not much adoration quenched communion?
> Must not Christ intend to restore communion?
> Now is your chance, Thomas, to serve Christ!
>
> CRANMER: I am God's servant and the King's.
> THE KING: Go then,
> and make me, as I am, irretrievably Anne's.

On the one side Henry, the absolute egoist and there-fore, except in his fundamental premise that he is the most important person in the universe, not a self-deceiver: he knows exactly what he wants. On the other, a man who at the deepest level is honest but torn by mixed feelings and motives about which he is not quite clear. As *Figura Rerum* is later to tell the audience:

> There is this to be said for my lord of Canterbury,
> he dimly believes in something outside himself –
> which is more, I can tell you, than most of you do.

and to Cranmer himself:

> Plastic, you sought integrity, and timid, courage.
> Most men, being dishonest, seek dishonesty;
> you, among few, honesty such as you knew,
> in corners of sin, round curves of deception . . .

In our age we are familiar with the case of the man, by nature a novelist or a poet, who has to decide whether he will devote himself to his art alone or become politically *engagé*. On this issue his conscience is genuinely divided: one voice tells him, quite correctly, that politics is a dirty business and that if he meddles with it, he will often have to compromise his artistic integrity; another voice tells him, equally correctly, that the cause of social justice is more important than the cause of art. And, as a rule, backing this second voice is a motive of which he is not conscious, the ambition of every man to shine in a field which is not his natural one – in the case of the artist, to come out of his cave and play a public role. Cranmer's case was the same. In addition, I think, his intellectual conviction of the Divine Right of Kings was emotionally reinforced by the admiration which a timid, retiring character often feels for a ruthless man of action like Henry.

After his acceptance of the Primacy, the audience's attention is diverted from Cranmer to the fate of Anne Boleyn. Each of us has an image of what is desirable to live for. In Henry's case this image had been temporarily embodied in Anne as the woman he was in love with and from whom he expected a male heir. His love faded and she gave birth to a daughter.

Finding that his image no longer corresponds to reality, Henry, like all egoists, regards it as her fault:

Thomas, Thomas, Anne is not what I thought.

On which *Figura Rerum* comments to the audience:

A remark few of you die without making,
nor shall you die without making . . .

Anne's image is simple enough:

I wanted so little:
only the Crown because it lay in my way,
and a few small pleasures – variations from Henry.

to which *Figura Rerum* replies:

If you had asked for the greatest conceivable things,
as Thomas does unintentionally, they would cost no more.
The price of heaven or hell or the world is similar –
always a broken heart, sometimes a broken neck.

Cranmer is sorry for her and tries in vain to save her, but his own image is too different for him to be able to understand either Henry or her. He puts his faith in learning and words. But, as *Figura Rerum* says:

Anne had an image of the Crown – she is dead;
it is sped, the image that the King had of Anne.
Are words wiser than women or worship? safer,
securer, purer? . . .

To hold high office under Henry was perilous, and most of those who did died on the scaffold. Cranmer's theological views were, from Henry's point of view, undoubtedly heretical, and if he had once lost favour with the King, he would have gone to the stake. Those who accuse him of being a cowardly time-server are unjust. It is true that, in his official capacity as Archbishop, he had to condemn to death as heretics men whose views were similar to his own and that he signed the Six Acts which imposed doctrines which he did not believe. But before signing them he had argued against them, both in Convocation and Parliament, a fact of which Henry must have been aware. In fact, Cranmer was denounced three times, first by the canons of his own cathedral, then in Parliament and then by the Lords Council, but each time Henry refused to listen to the charges. The egoist always assumes that the actions of all men are like his own, motivated by self-interest, a desire for power, glory, wealth, women, that their professed loyalty and affection is a sham – if they serve others it is because they think it is in their self-interest to serve. Since most men are egoists, he is usually right, and if, like Henry, he is an absolute monarch, a courtier who is not a self-seeker is a very rare exception indeed. Cranmer was the exception, as even his enemies admitted.

1ST LORD: A silly innocence lives in his face.
2ND LORD: It hath caught the King – unlike to unlike.
1ST LORD: Is he apt to be used?
2ND LORD: Apt to be used,
    being shy of his own heart and mind,
    but not so apt – none of his kind are –
    if you trouble his incalculable sense of honesty,
    which holds the King; who now has none,
    only a kind of clinging to honesty in others.

Whatever his motive for carrying out the orders of his King, even at the expense of his convictions, it was not self-interest. When the monasteries were dissolved, for example, he did not, as he very easily could have, and most of those about him did, acquire any of their wealth and lands. Nor when others fell out of favour with the King did he rejoice in their downfall and seek to profit from it; on the contrary, he pleaded mercy for them, for Anne, Fisher, More, Cromwell.

Henry, always a suspicious man and as he grew older pathologically so, knew that if he could trust any human being, it was Cranmer. He refused to listen to his enemies, and Cranmer was saved. Suppose he had listened, what would have happened? Would Cranmer have done as Shaxton, the Bishop of Salisbury, did at the time and he himself was to do ten years later – recant his views? It seems probable. But would he then have recanted his recantation? That seems less likely. *Figura Rerum* suggests that his escape is a double piece of luck. It is a visible mercy that he is spared here and now: it is an invisible mercy that he is spared the time to develop the spiritual strength to meet a test for which he is not yet prepared.

Henry now dies. Edward VI is a young boy, and the political power passes into the hands of a Regency made up of nobles belonging to the Protestant party, so that now Cranmer is free to make whatever doctrinal and ritual changes he believes to be necessary official policy. I do not know what the historical facts are, but Williams presents the Council as cynical men of the world who are interested only in power and regard Cranmer's religious concerns as a harmless, silly hobby.

Our bodies are made space and our blood time.
Enlarged so, a man's spirit has nothing,
nothing at all between himself and God.
Sacraments of nature are better than those of grace,
and a simple noble heart than copes and mitres.
But do not you trouble for that; go you
and use your patterns of words, versicles, responses,
formulae, vain repetitions, muttering and mummeries.

34

> We will deal with you at need as you deal with words;
> the King permits you to write your soul in words.

Cranmer was a priest and an artist, and, like all artistic priests, then and today, he overestimated the spiritual importance of liturgical reform and underestimated the resistance of the uneducated laity to it. Ritual is an immediate concern of the clergy because it is they who have to perform it every day. Thus, whether conservatives or reformers, they will give professional theological reasons why the rite should remain as it is or be altered, but the average layman clings to the ritual he is accustomed to, just as the mass followers of a political party do not notice when its leaders change their policies but would be outraged if they changed the traditional party vocabulary.

Cranmer introduced his reforms, and to his surprise the people actively revolted. As well-intentioned people often do when they encounter unexpected opposition, he lost his temper. He who had always been known for his kindness and concern for the poor now descends to plain abuse and addresses them thus:

> You ignorant rough creatures, you rocks and heaths,
> who will have the mystery of Christ to be no more
> than an unintelligible monster . . . because of my office
> and my duty to God and the King, now will I say
> what you should know and cannot: therefore hear.

on which *Figura Rerum* comments:

> How absolute we are! now in your night
> is there no ravage? does nothing, Thomas, roar
> like seas or winds or the crowds of the poor marching?
> is all hushed down to those sweet-sounding collects
> where reason and charity softly kiss each other?
> You were less certain in old days at Cambridge.

Those of us who are Anglicans know well that the language of the Book of Common Prayer, its extraordinary beauties of sound and rhythm, can all too easily tempt us to delight

in the sheer sound without thinking about what the words
mean or whether we mean them. In the General Confession,
for example, what a delight to the tongue and ear it is to
recite:

> We do earnestly repent and are heartily sorry for these our
> misdoings; the remembrance of them is grievous unto us;
> the burden of them is intolerable.

Is it really intolerable? Not very often.

So, in the play, when Cranmer has just written,

> It is very meet, right, and our bounden duty, that we
> should at all times and in all places, give thanks . . .

Figura Rerum says:

> Ah how the sweet words ring their beauty:
> *it is meet, right and our bounden duty.*
> But will you sing it with unchanged faces
> when God shall change the times and places?

And soon, for Cranmer, the time and place begin to
change. Edward VI is about to die, and Cranmer is seized
by fear and doubt:

> I sit in my study; a fit of fear takes my heart
> while in my mouth the grand art
> fails, speech fails . . .
> and the words in my book slither out of my sight . . .

The King dies and Mary becomes Queen. Why at this
point Cranmer did not, like most of his bishops, flee to the
Continent is, from the point of view of worldly common
sense, incomprehensible. There was nothing practical he
could do for the Protestant cause by staying. Yet he
stayed.

CRANMER: . . . I cannot fly. I will not turn from the things
     that I have done.
THE COMMONS: God save the Queen.

SKELETON: She is coming on you; you will lose your See.
CRANMER: It was given by God and the Prince, and it is theirs.

What did he expect to happen? Deposition, perhaps, but not a heretic's death:

> Have I erred? Let them show me then where I have erred.

To which *Figura Rerum* replies:

> In thinking, though it was important for you to be right, it mattered at all in the end whether you were right.

To liberal historians of the last century Cranmer's motive for recanting seemed simple: fear of being burned alive. Political events in this century have taught us that recantation can be more complicated. A convinced Marxist, committed to the view that the Communist Party is always right, rises to high position in the party and becomes its official theoretician. Suddenly the leaders of the party decide that there must be a switch in the party line; overnight his theories become Trotskyite, bourgeois or what-have-you. If he refuses to agree that his theories were wrong, then he must deny his basic premise that the party is always right. Substitute the Prince for the party, and the situation is Cranmer's.

QUEEN MARY: Will you recant?
CRANMER: I will always submit myself to the Church, and
  the Pope if the Pope be head of the Church,
  if they can prove me that out of the Scriptures.
QUEEN MARY: It shall not serve; will you submit yourself to
  adoration and our Father at Rome?
  We are the Prince, as our father was the Prince:
  will you set yourself up against us?
BISHOP: If the Pope is head of the Church, obey; if the Prince
  and the Prince admit the Pope, why, still obey.
  Will you set yourself up against your principles?

In desperation Cranmer makes an ambiguous answer:

If the Queen serve the Pope, I will serve the Queen.

The Queen sees through this:

> This shall not serve; we have signed the writ for the burning.

But the Bishop seems to promise that his life will be spared if he recants.

Now Cranmer is utterly alone in a dark night of physical terror and spiritual despair:

CRANMER: General Councils have erred and Popes have
erred:
   is it not like that my word went wrong?
SKELETON: It is like.
CRANMER: That when I strove at winning the land for Christ
   I erred from the beginning?
SKELETON: From the beginning.
CRANMER: Christ my God, I am utterly lost and damned.
   I sin whatever I do.
SKELETON: Whatever you do.
CRANMER: As well sin this way and live as that way and die.
   It is folly and misery all.
SKELETON: Folly and misery.
CRANMER: Did I sin in my mother's womb that I was forsaken
   all my life? Where is my God?
SKELETON: Where is your God?
   When you have lost him at last you shall come into God.
CRANMER: I will sign anything, everything. I have burned,
   and the flame is returned on my soul: if it saves from hell
   I may well recant; they may be right; they are,
   for they say they are, they are sure, they are strong.

He recants only to find that he has been tricked: they are going to burn him anyway. In the light of certain death, he realizes that he must die for what he has lived for, namely, words. In another play by Williams, *The House of the Octopus*, the hero Anthony can escape martyrdom if he will make a small compromise about language and says to himself:

38

The spirit matters
more than the letter. It were better to let slide
some jot or tittle, that has in its mere self
little significance than to split peace wide.
It is fit, if possible, not to antagonize souls
by the more-or-less, the give-and-take of words:
better that quarrels should cease, and peace live.

The Voice of the Holy Spirit corrects him:

It is, we of heaven agree, a thing indifferent; but any
indifference may become sometimes a test.
Will God dispute over words? no, but a man must, if
words mean anything, stand by words,
since stand he must; and on earth protest to death
against what at the same time is a jest in heaven.
Alas, you are not in heaven: the jests there
are tragedies on earth, since you lost your first poise
and crashed.

So, in recanting his recantation Cranmer stands by words:

. . . since the Queen will have me cut off from obedience,
outcast from her, I must have an outcast's mind,
a mind that is my own and not the Queen's . . .
Therefore I draw to the thing that troubles me
more than all else I ever did – the writings
I let abroad against my heart's belief
to keep my life . . . if that might be . . . that I signed
with this hand, after I was degraded; this hand,
which wrote the contrary of God's will in me,
since it offended most, shall suffer first;
it shall burn ere I burn, now I go to the fire. . . .

Williams has one more surprise in store for us. At the
very end, as Cranmer is leaving for the place of execution,
Figura Rerum demands one more admission.

SKELETON: Friend, let us say one thing more before the
world –
I for you, you for me: let us say all:
if the Pope had bid you live, you would have served him.

39

CRANMER: If the Pope had bid me live, I should have served
   him.

A drama, like any work of art, must obey the fundamental aesthetic law of interest. To be a viable subject for
a play the hero, whether a historical or a fictional figure,
must be somebody who holds our attention because what
he does or what happens to him is interesting, that is to
say, unusual. Furthermore, he must be exceptionally gifted
in his powers of speech, able to express what he feels and
thinks in a way which holds our attention. (Banality can
be made of comic interest but only by parodying it to the
point where the audience recognizes it as banality; but
exaggerated banality is no longer banal.) In the case of
the Epic Hero or the Tragic Hero, this presents no problem.
To be exceptional, to win immortal fame among men, is
the Epic Hero's *raison d'être*. The Tragic Hero wishes
bitterly that he is not an object of interest, but he knows
that the terrible and exceptional fate that has befallen
him will be remembered by men with wonder and terror.
The martyr, on the other hand, does not sacrifice his life
in order to be interesting, nor does he die with any
certainty that his death will in fact interest others; the
chances are that nobody will notice or remember it. Then
too it is a pure matter of chance, and irrelevant to his
being a martyr, if he can speak well or if he can only utter
banalities.

The dramatist who decides to write a play about someone
whose life ends in martyrdom is quite powerless to solve
this problem. He has no option but to choose someone
either like Becket or Cranmer, who played an exceptional
and interesting role in history, or like Celia in *The Cocktail
Party*, for whom he can invent an interesting history. He
can only hope against hope that his audience will have
the moral sophistication to sense what, as a dramatist, a
creator of secondary worlds, he is unable to say.

II

THE WORLD OF THE SAGAS

Present in every human being are two desires, a desire to know the truth about the primary world,* the given world outside ourselves in which we are born, live, love, hate and die, and the desire to make new secondary worlds of our own or, if we cannot make them ourselves, to share in the secondary worlds of those who can. Since we shall be concerned today with the human elements in the primary world on the one hand and with those secondary worlds which we call works of literature on the other, I shall personify the will-to-truth as the Historian, and the will-to-recreation as the Poet. The Historian cannot function without some assistance from the Poet, nor the Poet without some assistance from the Historian, but, as in any marriage, the question of who is to command and who to obey is the source of constant quarrels.

When we say that the primary world is the objective world outside ourselves, we mean that it is a social and public world. The criterion by which we judge 'outsideness' is social agreement. We believe that something is there outside our minds because our accounts of our individual sensory experiences agree. If I say that in the primary world all new leaves are green, I mean that the mental colour experience I call green is identical in all men except the colour-blind. The primary world contains every-

* For the terms 'primary' and 'secondary' worlds, I am indebted to Professor J. R. R. Tolkien's essay on fairy-tales.

thing that has not been made by man, including himself, and also whatever of man's historical past is still on hand as reified in a humanly fabricated world of languages, mythologies, legends, creeds, tools, works of art, etc. Though made by man, his past is no longer in his power to alter.

The Historian's questions – Is this true or false? Fact or fiction? Did this occur or did it not? – can be asked only of objects and events in the primary world. If a neighbour says to me, 'I met a dragon in the lane just now', my first thought will probably be, 'I must have misheard him.'

'What did you say?' I ask, and my suspicion is confirmed because now I hear him say, 'I met a waggon in the lane just now.' If, however, he did say 'dragon', I shall conclude that either he is mad or lying, since I do not believe that dragons exist in the primary world. But another possibility remains. He may be quoting a line of poetry. In that case, it is meaningless to ask whether the *words* are true or false. I can only ask, 'Is he quoting correctly or misquoting? Is the text of the poem from which he quotes correct or corrupt?'

Similarly, if a boy says to a girl, 'I love you', she may with good reason wonder if he really means what he says or is only pretending in order to seduce her, but if I read the lines:

> My dear and only love, I pray
> That little world of thee . . .

I cannot raise the question of sincerity: the words mean neither more nor less than they say.

I said just now that the most rigorous Historian cannot entirely dispense with the Poèt. In the first place, any history is already a secondary world, in that it can only be written or told in words, and the only elements in the primary world which language can exactly reproduce are the words that people speak there. It cannot describe all the physical properties of an object or all the temporal sequences of a motion or event. Language must abstract and select.

Secondly, if all the infinite variety of actual beings and events in the primary world, because equally actual, seemed equally significant to us, no history could be written at all. Luckily, they do not. For us, as for all living things, certain beings are of more concern to us than others because our survival depends upon them, objects which must be watched out for, fled from or fought. But also – and this, so far as we know, is peculiar to man – certain beings and events appeal, as we say, to our imagination, that is to say, irrespective of any practical importance they may have, they are felt to be sacred, enchanting, valuable in themselves. No Historian, however dispassionate he may try to be, can omit this fact without falsifying his picture of the human past.

On the other hand, if he did not experience such feelings of awe, wonder, enchantment in the primary world, I very much doubt if the Poet would desire or believe it possible to create secondary worlds. Being a man, not God, a Poet cannot create *ex nihilo*. If our desire to create secondary worlds arises at least in part from our dissatisfaction with the primary world, the latter must first be there before we can be dissatisfied with it. What in fact, then, are some of our principal grievances?

1. We are born into it and by death disappear from it without our consent. But the secondary worlds we make, since they are embodied in verbal or visual or auditory objects, come into being because we choose to make them and are not subject to natural death.
2. Our freedom of action, whether as individuals or as societies is very limited. In the secondary worlds we make we are omnipotent, with absolute freedom to say what they shall contain and what shall happen in them.
3. Our knowledge and understanding are very limited. In

43

a secondary world, we are omniscient, aware of everything which exists and happens in it and understanding exactly why.

4. Too many of our experiences are profane, unimportant, boring. From a secondary world we can exclude everything except what we find sacred, important, enchanting.

5. Evil and suffering are an insoluble problem. We can, if we wish, create Arcadian secondary worlds from which evil and suffering are excluded, but since, however unpleasant evil and suffering may be, nothing interests us more, most of the secondary worlds we create include them, but in a simplified more comprehensible form.

For instance, in fairy-tales instead of encountering, as we do in the primary world, human beings who are potentially good and evil, every one we meet is either good or evil and, except when under a spell, we cannot mistake one for the other, since the good are beautiful and speak finely and the evil ugly and coarse of speech. Further, while in the primary world evil so often appears to triumph over good, in the fairy-tale good is always ultimately victorious; the nice guys are rewarded, the bad guys punished.

When we compare works of literature, we find that we can assign them positions along, as it were, a spectrum, according to the part played in their composition by the Poet and the part played by the Historian. This spectrum is continuous, except that one can perhaps observe a critical point, on the one side of which the work is written in verse and on the other side in prose. A work written in verse at once proclaims its secondary character, since in the primary world human beings do not speak to each other in it.

Near the Historian's end of the spectrum come stories which, though they are fiction in that the persons and the events in them never existed and occurred, the reader is persuaded that they could have.

Let me take four examples from various points on this spectrum.

1. Shall I come, if I swim? Wide are the waves you see:
   Shall I come, if I fly, my dear love to thee?
   Streams Venus will appease; Cupid gives me wings:
   All the powers assist my desire,
   Save you alone that set my woeful heart on fire.

   You are fair, so was Hero that in Sestos dwelt;
   She a priest, yet the heat of love truly felt.
   A greater stream than this her love divide;
   But she was his guide with a light;
   So through the streams Leander did enjoy her sight.

   Thomas Campion

Campion's poem is about as far removed from the primary world as is possible without becoming unintelligible. That is to say, almost the only element he takes from the primary world is the English language. Sever that connection by translating the poem into another language, and it would make no sense at all. It does, perhaps, presuppose that the reader knows what love between the sexes is, but it cannot be called a love poem; the emotion has become purely verbal play; the four proper names in it refer to the myth of Hero and Leander, but if a reader does not know this myth, his ignorance will not, I think, be a serious obstacle to appreciating the poem. Appreciation depends upon having a poet's feeling for the rhythmical possibilities of the English language, which is increased if the reader recognizes the rules of the game: Campion is exploring the possibilities of applying classical prosody, scanned by syllable length, to English verse, scanned by accent.

2. The fair head fell from the neck to the earth and many pushed it with their feet where it rolled forth. The blood burst from the body and glistened on the green. Yet never faltered nor fell the hero for all that; but stoutly he started up with firm steps, caught his lovely head and lifted it up straightway. Then he turned his

45

steed, seized the bridle, stepped on his steel bow and
strode aloft, holding the head in the hand by the hair;
and as soberly the man sat in his saddle as if no mishap
had ailed him, though he was headless on the spot . . . he
held the head straight up in his hand, turned the face
towards the highest on the dais; and it lifted up the
eyelids and looked straight out, and spoke this much
with its mouth, as ye may now hear.

Gawain and the Green Knight

Here we are no longer in a purely verbal world. The words
are used in their concrete meanings derived from the
primary world to produce a sensory picture, but we know
at once that we are being told a tall story. Nobody, that is,
at any time, has believed that such an event could actually
take place, and the whole point would be lost if it was
believed that it could. The listener knows at once that he
is to enter the Perilous Realm of the fairy-story, a secondary
world of romantic knightly adventure, which, as Eric
Auerbach says, 'it is impossible to fit into any actual or
practically conceivable political system. It contains nothing
but the requisites of adventure, a world specifically
created and designed to give the knight opportunity to
prove himself.'

I presume you all have read *Gawain and the Green
Knight*, so I will not elaborate, except to remind you of the
role that the number three plays in it, the three scenes
between Gawain and his hostess, the three hunts. The
further removed from the primary world, the greater the
role played in it by magic numbers as an organizing
principle. It is not without reason, either, that poetry has
been called the Art of Numbers.

3. At once he went down from the rugged mountain with
   quick strides, and the long ridges and the woods trembled
   beneath the immortal feet of Poseidon as he passed.
   Three strides he made, and with the fourth he reached
   his goal, Aegea, where in the depths of the sea his
   glorious house is built, golden and glittering, inde-

structible for ever. There he came, and put to his
chariot his bronze-hoofed horses, swift-flying, with
manes of gold. He clad himself in gold and grasped a
well-wrought golden whip, and mounted his chariot
and set out across the waves. The creatures of the sea
arose on all sides, from the depths and gambolled near
him, nor did they fail to know their lord. With joy the
sea parted before him, and the horses flew right swiftly;
the bronze axle was not even wet beneath, and with
easy strides they bore him towards the ships of the
Achaeans.

Iliad

Even from a prose English translation the reader can
guess that the original Greek hexameters must be written
in a sublime style. The picture conjured up for the reader
is at once more detailed and more splendid than anything
in *Gawain*. Homer does not suggest, however, that any
Greek or Trojan actually witnessed what he describes.
But while the *Gawain* passage does not pretend to be
anything more than a tall story, Homer's lines could only
have been written in a society where the poet and his
audience believed that Poseidon really existed as one of
the supernatural inhabitants of the primary world, a God
to whom temples were raised and sacrifices made and to
whom the myths assigned certain properties, like a chariot
and horses. What he describes, so to speak, is what we
mortals would see if the immortals were always visible to
our sight, which they almost never are.

We readers today therefore, who are no longer poly-
theists, have to suspend our own beliefs and enter into the
Homeric world picture as if it were actual. As Historians
we can, of course, raise the questions: 'What is the historical
origin for belief in Poseidon? Why does a god of the sea
come to be associated with horses?' For all I know, Mr
Robert Graves may be right when he says:

The myth of Demeter and Poseidon records a Hellenic
invasion of Arcadia. Demeter was pictured at Phigalia as

47

the mare-headed patroness of the pre-Hellenic horse-cult. Horses were sacred to the moon, because their hooves make a moon-shaped mark, and the moon was regarded as the source of all water. The early Hellenes introduced a larger breed of horses into Greece from Trans-Caspia, the native variety having been about the size of a Shetland pony and unsuitable for chariotry. They seem to have seized the centres of the horse-cult, where their warrior kings forcibly married the local priestesses and thus won a title to the land.

But such speculations, however interesting and probable, are not of the slightest help to us in appreciating what Homer wrote.

4. Now they come at him, and he made a good and brave defence; he cut their pike-shafts through; there were stout strokes on both sides. And in that bout Eyjolf breaks his axe-heft, and catches up an oar, and then another, and both break with his blows. And in this bout Eyjolf gets a thrust under his arm, and it came home. Some say that he broke the shaft from the spear-head, and let it stay in the wound. He sees now that his defence is ended. Then he made a dash out and got through them before they knew. They were not expecting this; still they kept their heads, and a man named Mar cut at him and caught his ankle, so that his foot hung crippled. With that he rolls down the beach, and the sea was at the flood.

Sturlunga Saga

Reading this passage, we at once feel that the author claims our attention, not as an inventor of an entertaining tale, nor through the splendour of his verbal expression, but as the narrator of an event which actually happened in the primary world. The Historian's interest in truth is stronger than the Poet's love of form and patterning. For instance, 'Some say that he broke the shaft from the spear-head'. In the Poet's world no doubt is ever allowed as to whether what he says occurred. But in any actual event, how often eye-witnesses differ in their account, so that one cannot be exactly sure what happened. Again: 'A man named Mar cut at him and caught his ankle.' Who is this Mar? We have no idea. He emerges for a second as a person and then returns to the anonymous background from which he came. For a Poet, or even a prose writer like Henry James who takes a Poet's attitude towards narrative, how shockingly untidy. But, as we all know, the primary world is untidy, only capable, as James said, of splendid waste.

Here again two passages, this time not of description but reported dialogue. The first is from Book XXII of the *Iliad*. Hector has just received his death wound.

[HECTOR]

I beg you by your life, by your knees and by your parents, do not let the dogs of the Achaeans devour me beside the ships, but accept ample gold and bronze, the gifts my father and my queenly mother will give to you, and give my body back home, that the Trojans and the Trojans' wives may give me in death the meed of fire.

[ACHILLES]

Dog, beseech me neither by my knees nor by my parents. Would that my angry heart would let me cut off your raw flesh and eat it, for what you have done to me. There is none who could ward off the dogs from your head, not though they bring ten and twenty times your ransom and weigh it out here and promise yet more besides; not even though Dardanian Priam should buy your weight in gold, not even so shall your queenly mother lay you in your bed and weep for you she bore herself, but the dogs and birds shall devour you utterly.

[HECTOR]

Well do I know you as I look upon you; there was no hope that I could move you for surely your heart is iron in your breast. Take care now lest I be the cause of anger of the gods against you on that day when Paris and Phoebus Apollo shall slay you for all your valour at the Scaen Gates.

What Hector and Achilles say is consonant with their characters and appropriate to the situation they are in, but no one will seriously imagine that he is listening to speeches that could have taken place. No two warriors, one of them dying, the other exhausted by battle, could speak, like orators with their speeches prepared, at such a length and with every clause in the right place. Homer is creating a typical Poet's world in which nothing remains hidden but all is manifest. What a hero says and the style in which he says it must be the verbal reflection of his heroic deeds, and nothing which he can be imagined as wishing to say must remain unsaid.

The second passage is from the seventy-seventh chapter of the Njal Saga.*

> Now Gunnar received two wounds himself. He said to Hallgerd: 'Let me have two locks of your hair, and help my mother plait them into a bow-string for me.'
>
> 'Does anything depend upon it,' asked Hallgerd.
>
> 'My life depends upon it, for they will never overcome me as long as I can use my bow.'
>
> 'In that case, I shall now remind you of the slap in the face you once gave me. I do not care in the least whether you hold out a long time or not.'
>
> 'To each his own way of earning fame. You shall not be asked again.'

Here both in style and in length, the dialogue is credible as an actual conversation in the circumstances. Further, Hallgerd's reply to Gunnar's request is as unexpected and astonishing to the reader as it is to Gunnar himself.

We have, to be sure, been told in Chapter 48 about

---

* The extracts from *Njal's Saga* (Penguin Classics) on pp. 50, 52–4, 60–1 and 62–5, are reprinted by permission of Penguin Books Ltd and the translators, Mr Magnus Magnusson and Mr Hermann Palsson.

Gunnar slapping her face, but this occurred at least six years previously. Much has happened meanwhile: the incident has never been mentioned again; their married life has continued as if nothing had happened; we, like Gunnar, have forgotten about it, and it is only now that we learn that Hallgerd has never forgotten. Such a concealment would not, I think, be possible in Homer. Penelope may conceal her feelings from the suitors, but the reader knows what they are and is not allowed to forget them.

Both the examples I have cited of a literature in which the Historian is predominant over the Poet are taken from the Icelandic prose sagas, and I shall devote the rest of my lecture to them. As examples of what I would call Social Realism (not to be confused either with socialist realism or naturalism), they are astonishing for two reasons.

First, their date. The earliest manuscripts date from about 1300, which means that the essential characteristics of the kind of literature they represent must have been discovered much earlier. Nothing like them, so far as I know, had ever been attempted in western literature before, and in the rest of Europe nothing similar can be found before the end of the eighteenth century.

Second, their excellence. I do not think that in what they set out to do even the greatest realistic novelists of the nineteenth century have surpassed them. It may be admitted that the primary world of tenth-century Iceland – its scale, its ways of life, its values, its interests – was easier to depict than the primary world of an urban and industrialized society, but the originality and excellence of the sagas is still a miracle. The Icelandic writers had so mastered the art of realistic narrative that it was only in 1949 that the Hrafnkels Saga was discovered to be purely fictitious; till then all scholars had previously believed it to have a historical basis.

The Historian, or Social Realist, begins by asking: 'What do I know for certain about my fellow human beings?' and his answer is: 'What they do and say in the presence of others who can bear witness to it. I may be able to make plausible guesses about their unspoken thoughts, but guesses are not evidence, so I must exclude them. How is a person or a deed in the primary world to be morally judged? By the standards of the community to which the doer belongs. I may, indeed I must, report the kind of moral reputation my characters enjoy and how their actions are judged by public opinion. My own moral values may be different, and I may be convinced that they are superior, but I must exclude them and leave it to my readers to pass judgement, if they care to.'

Similarly, when considering the motives of human beings for their actions, the Historian will say, 'I must confine myself to what is public knowledge. I may and should report the reason a man gives for acting in a certain way, if he gives one: but if he remains silent, I am not entitled to assign him a motive myself, however convinced I may be that I knew it. I can and should report the motives attributed to him, by his neighbours, but I must report these as their conclusions without comment.'

Finally, in his picture of the primary world the Historian must be continually on his guard against the desire of the Poet inside himself for idealistic simplification.

In a poetic world (the world of the *Iliad* for example) outward appearances are exact manifestations of inner characteristics; it is unthinkable that a Homeric hero should have any physical blemish. In the world of the sagas the relation between outside and inside is more ambiguous. Skarp-Hedin, one of the greatest warriors in the Njal Saga, is described thus:

> He had curly chestnut hair and handsome eyes. His face was very pale and his features sharp. He had a crooked nose and prominent teeth which made him ugly round the mouth. He looked every inch a warrior.

The Poet would have human beings absolute embodiments

of a virtue or a vice. A man should be either absolutely brave or absolutely cowardly. Consequently, if the Poet is forced to admit that, on a particular occasion, one of his brave heroes behaves timidly, he has to attribute this to divine intervention. The Historian, on the other hand, while admitting that some men are brave and some cowards, recognizes that many, perhaps most, men are both brave and cowardly to a certain degree, depending upon circumstances. In the Njal Saga we are introduced to a minor character, Bjorn the White, of whom we are told:

> Bjorn was always bragging about himself, which his wife disliked intensely. He was keen-sighted and good at running.

When Kari is thinking of enlisting his help Bjorn's wife warns him:

> Don't rely on Bjorn's manhood, for I'm afraid that he'll prove less courageous than he makes out.

The braggart *miles gloriosus* is a stock figure in fiction, and the reader naturally expects that, when it comes to a test, Bjorn will be exposed as a comic poltroon. What actually happens is much more interesting. Kari and Bjorn find themselves about to be attacked by a gang of enemies. Kari says:

> There are two courses open to you. You can either stand behind me with a shield to protect yourself with, if it is any use to you, or you can mount your horse and ride away as fast as you can.

To this, Bjorn replies:

> I certainly don't want that, and for several reasons. In the first place, it could be that malicious tongues might suggest that I abandoned you out of cowardice if I rode away. In the second place, I know what a catch they would think me, and two or three of them would ride after me, and I would be of no use or help to you then.

So Bjorn stays and, though it is Kari who has to do most of

53

the fighting, he does manage to wound three men. On their way home afterwards he says to Kari:

> Now you must be a real friend to me when I meet my wife, for she won't believe a word I tell her. This is of vital importance to me. Repay me now for the fine support I have given you.

Thus, while Bjorn is depicted as a somewhat ridiculous figure, vain and henpecked, he is not made contemptible.

All art is gratuitous, so that one can never say that a certain kind of society must necessarily produce a certain kind of art. On the other hand, when we consider a certain society and the literature which it actually did produce, we can sometimes see reasons why it was possible for such a society to produce it. If the realism of the sagas is unique for its time, the Icelanders and their society were in many ways unique too.

The Norsemen who colonized Iceland were of aristocratic stock, and their reason for coming to Iceland was that they did not want to be ruled by, or owe allegiance to, any king or superior. They came not in a host led by a commander but one by one, as individuals or families who regarded each other as equals, and the island they came to was uninhabited.

Consequently, the social situation, normal in most of the west, of warriors invading a country and making its previous inhabitants an inferior and subject race was absent. Most of the island was uninhabitable, so that the number of people it could support was limited – when the colonizing period ended, the population numbered at most 60,000 – and the fertile parts were so scattered that no large estates and no cities were possible.

Then, though some of the colonizers brought slaves with them, there were never enough of these to constitute a slave class.

The combination of these factors created, for the first and last time in civilized history, a rural democracy:

elsewhere democracy has always been an urban phenom-
enon. It is not difficult to see why such conditions make a
literature of Social Realism possible and might even
suggest the idea of writing it. In a society where everybody
knows everybody else at first hand, and what anybody
does or says very soon gets known to everybody else, pure
fantasy is possible, but partial manipulation of historical
facts will displease an audience that knows the real ones.
Again, in a small almost classless society, and only in
such, it is possible to portray realistically the whole of
society. In a society where the lower classes, slaves, subject
peasants, etc., are not considered persons in their own
right and therefore not worth looking at, or in an urban
culture where few people know each other by sight or
name, only one's own class or one's personal friends can be
realistically described, and even then the picture is bound
to be false, for no class or intimate circle exists in a
vacuum without relations to other classes and strangers,
which are an important factor in their social reality; yet
these relations cannot be realistically portrayed.

Linguistically, also, the Icelanders were unique among
the societies of their time in that they all spoke, as they
still do to this day, a *Hochsprache:* there was no difference
between cultured and vulgar speech, nor between the
spoken and the written language. Further, its syntactical
nature made it an excellent medium for realistic prose
narrative. Greek and Latin, with their wealth of devices
for organizing facts, their conjunctions, their graded tenses,
make them admirable media for poetry and for formal
oratory, but their very virtues are a disadvantage when it
comes to reporting a rapid succession of events or informal
conversation, for they tempt the writer to over-organize
his material, to make a too tidy whole out of a world
where heterogeneity and accident are essential elements
in its reality.

Professor Auerbach has demonstrated the beneficial
effect upon the Latin of the early Christian writers of the

biblical use of parataxis. Of a phrase in St Augustine's *Confessions, aperuit ocules et percussus est*, he says:

> This would be impossible in classical Latin where one would find a causal or at least a temporal hypotaxis. Yet this procedure, far from weakening the interdependence of the two events brings it out more emphatically, just as in English it is more dramatically effective to say: he opened his eyes and was struck, than to say: When he opened his eyes, or, upon opening his eyes, he was struck.

Parataxis comes naturally to Icelandic. A. C. Bouman has analysed a number of the sagas and finds, for example, that:

> The ratio of parataxis to hypotaxis in the narrative portions ranges from 60 per cent or more in Njal's Saga, Gislasaga, Heiarviga, and Dropla Droplauga to less than 50 per cent in Laxdaela, Egil and Grettir. The oldest sagas seem to have the greatest percentage of parataxis.

If their poetry and prose is an accurate reflection of their characters, then one of the most striking differences between the Norsemen and both the Greeks and the Romans is their different attitude towards fine rhetoric and forensic oratory. The Icelanders seem to have been passionately interested in law and litigation, but their interest was technical rather than literary. What they really enjoyed was winning an apparently hopeless case by finding a legal loophole; we never hear of someone winning a case through a fine speech which sweeps the court off its feet. I think there is only one place in the sagas where a long speech is quoted verbatim. In the Grettir saga we are told that Haf, son of Thor, was a man of many words, after which we are given his speech, which is evidently intended to be a parody of purple prose.

Certain characteristics both of the earlier epic poems and of the later court poetry of the Skalds, whether derived from the language itself or from the poetic tastes of the Norsemen, partially explain why, when they reached the point of wanting to narrate a story, they chose prose rather than verse as a medium.

Unlike most Anglo-Saxon epic poetry, the poems in the Elder Edda are written in strophes with end-stopped lines, so that the movement is lyrical rather than narrative. Furthermore, the poets, instead of relating their mythical subjects in full detail, assume that those listening already know it. What they concentrate upon are not the events but the dramatic monologues or dialogues of the characters involved in them. By the time the poems came to be written down, the scribes evidently felt that the average reader could no longer be expected to get all the allusions, for in a number of cases they added a prose gloss. Unlike the Greeks, the peoples of Northern Europe seem to have been fascinated by poetic riddles. The kennings so common in their poetry are, like the epithets in Homer, metrical formulae, but unlike the latter, their meaning is not self-evident. As an example of this poetry, here is an extract from *The Lay of Völund*, as translated by Paul B. Taylor and myself.

> Long he sat till asleep he fell;
> What he knew when he woke was not joy:
> He saw on his hands heavy chains,
> His feet in fetters were fast bound.

> 'Who are the men who my hands have chained?
> Who have fettered my feet together?'

> Then the Lord of the Njars, Nidud, answered:
> 'What good have you gotten, greatest of elves,
> From our treasure, Völund, in Wolfdale?'

Then said Völund:

> 'Was there not gold on Grani's Road?
> Far thought I our realm from the Rhine hills.
> Greater treasure we had in olden days,
> At home in the hall, happy together,

Hladgud and Hervor, Hlödver's children,
And wise-counselling Ölrun, Kjar's daughter.'

Prose gloss: Nidud the king gave his daughter, Bödvild,
the gold ring he had taken from the beast at Völund's.
And he himself wore the sword which had been Völund's.

Without stood the wily one, wife of Nidud,
In she came through the end door,
Stood there smiling and softly whispered:
'Woeful shall he be who from the wood comes.'

He gnashes his teeth when he notices the sword,
And on Bödvild's arm beholds his ring.
His eyes glare, grim as a snake's:
With a knife they cut his knee-sinews,
Set him on the island of Saevarstöd.

From the verses alone, without the help of the prose
gloss, the lines

He gnashes his teeth when he notices the sword,
And on Bödvild's arm beholds his ring.

would be unintelligible. It was told in an earlier verse
that Nidud's men took away a ring, but no sword was
mentioned. When the name Bödvild appears for the first
time, we have never been told who she is. Again, while
the epithet Homer applies to Diomedes, 'of-the-loud-war-
cry', is straightforward description, no reader could guess
that the kenning 'Grani's Road' means the river Rhine,
unless he already knows the Völsung legend in which
Grani is the name of Sigurd's horse, and Sigurd journeys
down the Rhine.

When we come to the Skaldic poetry the difficulties
have become infinitely greater. The kennings are even
more erudite, and, as in Irish and Welsh poetry, the
technical complications of the verse forms are so formidable
that one is surprised that the poets succeeded in saying
anything. Certainly, it is absolutely impossible to translate

them and remain in any way faithful to the metre. The formal rules of the *drottkvaett*, for example, are as follows.

It is a stanza of four couplets. Each line has three stresses and ends on an unaccented syllable. The first line of each couplet has two alliterations and an assonance; the second is related to the first by alliteration and also contains an internal rhyme. Last, the ordinary names for things should be replaced by kennings.

The following example, written by me, is, I trust, fairly correct, though I had to ignore the unaccented ending rule.

> Hushed is the lake of hawks,
> Bright with our excitement,
> And all the sky of skulls
> Glows with scarlet roses;
> The melter of men and salt
> Admires the drinker of iron;
> Bold banners of meaning
> Blaze o'er our host of days.

It is clear that in such verse it would be absolutely impossible to tell a story. Sagas, if composed at all, would have to be written in prose.

To demonstrate what I mean by their Social Realism, I shall, in the short time at my disposal, have to confine myself to two matters: the conversion of Iceland to Christianity, as told in the Njal and Laxdaela sagas, and the story of the love between Gudrun and Kjartan, as told in the Laxdaela Saga. I have selected these because, judging from western literature as a whole, religion and love are the two subjects about which writers have found it hardest to be objective and realistic.

The Laxdaela Saga describes the conversion from paganism to Christianity of a single individual, Kjartan. In most early accounts of such an event the conversion is effected either by a miracle or by the words and example of a holy man, and the result is a revolutionary change in the behaviour of the convert; before, he led a worldly lascivious life; after, he gives away his possessions and becomes a celibate ascetic. Nothing like this happens to Kjartan.

He arrives in Norway, the king of which is Olaf Tryggvason, a great warrior and a fanatical Christian whose method of converting his subjects is quite simple; 'Either', he says to them, 'you become Christians or I shall kill you.' The saga, incidentally, makes no attempt to gloss over this, though it does – with what historical justification I don't know – credit him with remarkable powers of insight into the minds of others.

Kjartan's first encounter with Olaf is in the water, where they are both swimming. Without knowing who his opponent is, Kjartan engages the stranger in a ducking-match and finds to his surprise that, for the first time in his life, he has met his equal in physical strength. Naturally, this gives him a favourable impression of Olaf, but when he realizes that the king may try to convert him and his fellow Icelanders by force he makes a plan to burn the king inside his hall. Olaf gets wind of this and asks Kjartan if it is true. Kjartan admits it. Olaf behaves magnanimously.

> Since I don't know whether your heart was in what you said, and since you have owned to it like a man, I shall not take your life. It may also very well be that you who have spoken more against the faith than the others will keep it more. And it is my guess, Kjartan, that you will have a better faith when you sail from Norway than when you came here.

In thanking the king for sparing their lives, Kjartan says:

> Certainly you can best tempt us into accepting the new faith by giving up serious charges against us and speaking to us in this friendly manner. But to this extent only do I intend to accept the faith in Norway. I'll put but little stock in Thor next winter when I get back to Iceland.

60

Then the king smiled and said: One can see from the looks of Kjartan that he thinks he has better reason to put trust in his own strength and weapons than in Odin and Thor.

Next Christmas Kjartan attends a sermon given by Olaf and decides to become a Christian:

So much [he says] did I like the king the first time I saw him that I knew at once he was a most outstanding man, and later, whenever I saw him at gatherings of men, this has always held good. And yet I like him much the best today, and I surmise that our whole welfare lies in our believing Him to be the True God whom the king proclaims.

Kjartan, that is to say, is converted because Olaf, the Christian, displays the epic virtues of martial prowess and magnanimity to a greater degree than any pagan he knows.

Olaf suggests to him that he return to Iceland and convert the country, by force if necessary. Kjartan is unwilling to do this and asks to stay in the King's service. Knowing both Olaf's character and his reputation for ferocity, he uses an argument which seems more worldly than pious:

As far as my father and other chieftains who are closely related to me, I dare say it will not be more difficult to bring them round to your bidding when I am under your power.

When he does return to Iceland, conversion has made one change in his behaviour:

Kjartan kept dry fast during Lent; and thus did what no man had ever done before him in this country. People thought it so strange that Kjartan lived such a long time meatless that they came long distances just to look at him.

But otherwise, at least to the outward eye, his way of life, his actions, his scale of values remain exactly what they were before.

In an account of the conversion of a society we also expect to be told that it was the work of preachers inspired by the Holy Spirit whose words stir the hearts of their hearers to repent and receive the Gospel gladly; we expect the preacher's words to be confirmed by spectacular miracles; and we expect those who reject the Gospel and persecute its ministers and converts to be portrayed as wicked men possessed by the Devil and to be told that they came to a bad end.

According to the *Landesbok*, most of the first settlers who came to Iceland, not directly from Norway but by way of Ireland and the Hebrides, were Christians but

> in few cases did this pass from parents to progeny, for the sons of some of these men reared Temples and did sacrifices. At the same time we are told of a man named Hall the godless. He was the son of Helgi the godless; neither father nor son would sacrifice, but they trusted in their own might.

Whether, a hundred years later, there were any of these original Christians left the Njal Saga does not say, but it is obvious that on their travels many Icelanders had come into contact with Christians, and some, like Njal himself, were favourably impressed.

> Njal heard many people say that it was monstrous to forsake the old beliefs. But Njal replied: 'In my opinion the new faith is much better; happy the man who receives it. And if the men who spread this faith come out to Iceland, I shall do all I can to further it.'

There must also have been a number who, while officially pagan, had, like Helgi and his son, lost their belief in the old gods.

The first missionaries sent to Iceland by King Olaf were Thangbrand and Gudleif Arason, both of them formidable warriors. One miracle is recorded of Thangbrand, but this is balanced by a pagan miracle. The sorcerer Hedinn causes the ground to burst open under Thangbrand's horse. Thangbrand just manages to save himself, but his horse and gear are swallowed up.

In the minds of those he meets the questions generally seem to be: which is the strongest, the Christian God or the old gods? Which are most likely to bring me luck? Thus Hall of Sida decides to be baptized after the following dialogue:

[HALL]

In whose honour are you celebrating this day?

[THANGBRAND]

The angel Michael.

[HALL]

What power has this angel?

[THANGBRAND]

Great power. He weighs everything you do, both good and evil, and he is so merciful that the good weighs more heavily with him than the evil.

[HALL]

I would like to have him for my friend.

[THANGBRAND]

You can do that easily. Give yourself to him in God's name this very day.

[HALL]

I want you to stipulate that you pledge your word on his behalf that he shall become my guardian angel.

[THANGBRAND]

I give you my promise.

Thangbrand, whose ship has lately been wrecked, has less success, however, with Steinun, the mother of the poet Ref.

[STEINUN]

Did you ever hear how Thor challenged Christ to a duel, and Christ did not dare accept the challenge?

63

[THANGBRAND]

I have heard that Thor would be nothing but dust and ashes if God did not permit him to live.

[STEINUN]

Do you know who wrecked your ship?

[THANGBRAND]

What do you think?

[STEINUN]

It was Thor's giant-killing hammer
That smashed the ocean-striding Bison . . .
Your Christ could not save
This buffalo of the sea from destruction:
I do not think your God
Kept guard over him at all.

Thangbrand makes some converts, but becomes discouraged and returns to Norway.

Thangbrand discussed with Guest whether he should travel west to the Fjords. Guest advised against it and said that the people there were hard and unpleasant to deal with. And, he said, if it is fated that this new faith be accepted, it will be accepted at the Althing, and all the chieftains from every district will be present.

When the question is raised at the Althing, it looks as if the division between the Christians and pagans might lead to civil war:

Next day both sides went to the Law Rock, named witnesses, and renounced their community of laws. The Law Rock was in such an uproar that no one could make himself heard. People then dispersed and everyone thought the situation looked very ugly. The Christians chose Hall of Sida to be their law-speaker, but Hall went to see Thorgeir the Priest of Ljoswater and gave him three marks of silver to proclaim what the law should be. It was taking a risk, for Thorgeir was a heathen.

After meditating for twenty-four hours, Thorgeir spoke:

64

'It seems to me that an impossible situation arises if we do not all have one and the same law. If the laws are divided, the peace will be divided, and we cannot tolerate that. Now, therefore, I want to ask the heathens and the Christians whether they will accept the law which I am going to proclaim.'

They all agreed. Thorgeir insisted on oaths and binding pledges from them. They all agreed to that, and gave their pledge. Then he said: 'The first principle of our laws is that all men in this land shall be Christian and believe in the one God and renounce all worship of idols. They shall not expose children at birth, nor eat horse-flesh. The penalty for carrying on these practices openly shall be outlawry, but they shall not be punishable if they are done in private.'

The heathens felt that they had been grossly betrayed, but despite that, the new faith became law, and the whole land Christian.

The saga, that is, makes it quite plain that Christianity was officially adopted for political, not theological, reasons and leaves it to the reader to guess how much Thorgeir's decision was affected by the money he had been given by the Christian party. When one remembers that the sagas were almost certainly put into writing by clerics, such objectivity seems astonishing.

Tales of tragic love can be found both in Greek and Norse mythology. One, perhaps the most popular, tragic situation is the loving woman deserted by the unloving or unfaithful man. For this she may take revenge – like Medea, by killing his children or, like Brynhilde, by persuading others to kill him – or, like Dido, she may kill herself. In other tales the love is mutual, but circumstances over which they have no control bring it to a tragic end. Their parents and a misunderstanding about a lion cause Pyramus and Thisbe to kill themselves; Leander gets accidentally drowned. Yet another theme is the two sworn friends who, having fallen in love with the same woman, have a fatal quarrel. In this case, too, the love is one-sided, for the interest lies in the relation between the two rivals, not in the feelings, if any, entertained by the woman.

By the time the Laxdaela Saga was written the cult of courtly love had already been invented in Provence and was soon to be spread all through Europe in the verse and prose romances. The most famous stories produced by this cult are the legend of Launcelot and Guinevere and the legend of Tristan and Isolde. The basic doctrines of the cult were:

> Love is impossible between a married couple. It can only exist where there is some barrier between the lovers, and the usual barrier is the marriage of the woman to another man. The love between them is all-absorbing, the only thing in their lives that matters. At all moments they must be thinking of each other and of nobody else. The man, to be sure, may go on knightly adventures, but it is solely for his beloved's sake that he undertakes them. Infidelity in deed or even in thought is unthinkable. Lastly, comedy and bawdry are for the lower orders, villains who are incapable of love.

The position of women in Icelandic society, as depicted in the sagas, will, I think, surprise most readers. In the first place, compared with women in Greek or Roman society or societies on the mainland of Europe during the early Middle Ages, they seem to have enjoyed an exceptional freedom. Though their marriages were often arranged by their parents, they could divorce an unsatisfactory spouse with little difficulty. Secondly, Icelandic husbands seem to have been absolutely incapable of keeping their wives in order. It is nearly always the women who are responsible for initiating a quarrel between families and, time and time again, when the men are trying desperately to end a blood feud peaceably by financial settlements, it is their wives who goad them on to more killing.

In the Laxdaela Saga the relationship between Kjartan and Gudrun is only one theme among many. When we are first told of a meeting between them the saga is more than half over, and after Kjartan's death there are still fifty chapters to go.

When Kjartan meets Gudrun she has already been married twice. At 15 she was married off against her will to a wealthy coward whom she despised. One of their neighbours was a man, Thord, who had married for her money a woman whom he did not love.

> Gudrun showed little love for Thorvald and was hard to please when it came to buying finery. There was no trinket in all the Westfjords so dear that Gudrun did not think she ought to have it, and she paid Thorvald back with ill-temper if he did not buy it, no matter how costly it was. Thord Ingusnarson got in thick with Thorvald and Gudrun and spent much of his time with them, and people often hinted at a love affair between Gudrun and Thord.

Whether this rumour was true or false, Gudrun and Thord, by using somewhat underhand legal tricks, succeeded in divorcing their respective spouses and married each other, and the saga says: 'Their married life went well.' Two years later, Thord is drowned at sea.

The theme of the wife who revenges herself upon the husband she has been compelled to marry by being recklessly extravagant is quite common in literature, but only in comedy. Such behaviour, however natural, is not expected of tragic heroines. So too with the divorces, which are comically ingenious but not exactly noble or courtly. In courtly romance the fact that her second marriage is a success would deprive her, I think, of any right to the privilege of a tragic love later.

When they meet, Kjartan is a bachelor, Gudrun a

widow, so that there is no external obstacle to their marriage. Kjartan is the handsomest man in Iceland, Gudrun the most beautiful woman. They have fallen in love with each other and, if not officially engaged, have come to an understanding: the whole community knows of this and thoroughly approves.

The fatal obstacle is not external but within themselves: each wishes for a proof of affection by asking the other to make a sacrifice, but out of pride, a fear of appearing the submissive one, neither will give this proof.

It is natural that Kjartan, a young man, should want to travel abroad by himself before settling down to married life; it is equally natural that Gudrun, as a woman, once she is certain of her own feelings, should want to get married as soon as possible.

Kjartan rode to Laugar and told Gudrun about his going abroad. 'You have made a rather hasty decision, Kjartan,' Gudrun said, and she added a few words from which Kjartan could gather that she felt displeased about it. Kjartan said: 'Don't be annoyed over this. I shall do something else to make it right with you.' Gudrun answered; 'Hold to your promise, for I can tell you now what I want.' Kjartan asked her to do so. Gudrun said: 'I want to go abroad with you this summer. Then you will more than have made up for your rash decisions, for I don't like it here in Iceland.' 'That cannot be,' said Kjartan, 'your brothers are still young and your father is old. If you leave the country, they will be without anyone to look after them. But wait for me three years.' Gudrun said she would make no such promise, and each would only see it their way.

Kjartan and his bosom friend, his foster-brother Bolli, go to Norway. While they are there Kjartan and the king's sister, Ingibjorg, become greatly attached to each other. Bolli notices this, and when he is about to return to Iceland, leaving Kjartan behind, he remarks, with an obvious reference to Gudrun:

I take it for granted that you recall very little those pleasures which are to be had in Iceland, when you are sitting talking to Ingibjorg, the King's sister.

Kjartan gives him an ambiguous answer:

Don't be saying such things, but bear my greetings to kinsmen and friends alike.

He does not, that is to say, send any special message to Gudrun, but his words imply that he does not want her to hear of Ingibjorg's existence. Bolli, however, does tell her:

He said that it was his guess that the king would rather give Ingibjorg to him in marriage than let Kjartan go. Gudrun said that was all good news 'for Kjartan will only be worthily matched if he gets a fine woman'. With this she abruptly let their talk drop and went away and was scarlet in the face.

Now we learn for the first time that Bolli is also in love with Gudrun, for he proposes to her. One cannot, however, call his telling her about Ingibjorg a base betrayal of his friend. Though he naturally hopes that Kjartan is going to marry Ingibjorg, he honestly believes that this is more likely than not, for, as he says to Gudrun:

He would have had a chance to entrust this matter to me, had it meant very much to him.

To make sure that we do not judge Bolli too harshly, the saga describes the parting scene between Kjartan and Ingibjorg. She has learned of Gudrun's existence and sadly realizes that Kjartan loves her more than herself, but the parting is not so easy for him either.

Ingibjorg brought out a white headdress worked in gold. 'It no doubt will be good enough for Gudrun Osvifsdottir to wrap around her head and you can give it to her as a wedding gift. Now farewell and luck be with you.' After that Kjartan stood up and gave her a kiss. And if truth be told, people thought it hard for them to part.

When Bolli proposes to Gudrun, she turns him down, and tells him frankly:

> There's no use talking about such a thing, Bolli. I will marry no one as long as Kjartan is alive.

Bolli, however, foolishly persists in his wooing despite the warnings of his foster-father, who reminds him:

> It is certainly no less known to you, Bolli, than to me, what talk there has been concerning the love between Kjartan and Gudrun.

And Gudrun, equally foolishly, finally yields – presumably her pride cannot endure being talked about as a woman who has been left by her lover for another. In a small community the Ingibjorg story had got around, and she cannot endure the thought of being whispered about.

They get married, and we are told:

> There was not much love lost in Bolli and Gudrun's married life, at least not on Gudrun's part.

When Kjartan returns and learns of the marriage his feelings, though he tries to hide them, are violent, but he does none of the things which are conventional in love stories. He neither challenges Bolli to single combat, nor retires to a monastery. Instead he marries another woman, Hrefna, and, contrary to all convention, the saga tells us that Kjartan and Hrefna came to love each other very much. This does not mean that his love for Gudrun has vanished. On one occasion Hrefna taunts him about it:

> Kjartan turned very red at this – and it was plain for everyone to see that he was angry she made such sport of him. 'Nothing of what you say, Hrefna, has come before my eyes. Besides Gudrun would not need to deck herself out in the headdress in order to look lovelier than all other women.' With that Hrefna broke off talking.

It will be remembered that, when she first heard of Ingibjorg, Gudrun too turned red in the face.

Kjartan's marriage does, however, set in motion the train of events which will end in bloodshed. Gudrun is, unreasonably but understandably, furious. But what she does first, and what Kjartan does in return, are acts which violate every convention of heroic or romantic literature. Heroes and Heroines may kill each other or themselves, but they cannot steal; only villains are capable of theft. Yet when Kjartan and Hrefna are paying a visit to Gudrun's father his sword and her headdress disappear, obviously at Gudrun's instigation. Kjartan revenges himself by doing something which literary convention confines to ribald farce:

> That winter after Yule, Kjartan gathered some men together, sixty in all. He took along tents and provisions and continued on his way until he came to Laugar. He ordered his men to dismount and told some of them to look after the horses and others to put up the tents. It was customary at that time to have an outdoor privy, some distance from the house, and so it was at Laugar. Kjartan stationed guards at all the doors of the farm house and barred the exit of all persons, so that they had to relieve themselves indoors for three days and nights. After that Kjartan rode home to Hjardarholt and his followers went their own ways.

Gudrun is so enraged by this incident that she forces Bolli against his will to kill Kjartan, his best friend. Then Kjartan's mother stirs up his brothers till they avenge his death by slaying Bolli. Here the saga follows heroic models, in particular the legend of Sigurd and Brynhilde. The style becomes more elevated but without losing contact with the primary world. Though the following dialogue must have been invented by the author of the saga, for it is difficult to see how anyone could have overheard it, it still remains credible as an actual conversation:

> Gudrun said: The seeds of discontent have certainly borne great fruit. I have spun twelve ells of yarn, and you have killed Kjartan. Bolli answered: It's going to take a long

enough time as it is for me to forget that mishap without your having to remind me of it. Gudrun said: Such a thing I would not count among mishaps. It seemed to me that you enjoyed greater esteem that winter when Kjartan was in Norway than afterwards when he returned to Iceland and trod you underfoot. And last, but not least, what means the most to me is that Hrefna will not be laughing when she goes to bed tonight. Then Bolli replied and was exceedingly angry: I have my doubts that she will turn any more pale at these tidings than you, and I'm not so sure but what it would have been a lesser shock to you if we all were lying on the ground and Kjartan had brought you the news.

When Bolli gets killed in turn Gudrun appears not to care very much, which, after what we have been told about their marriage, does not surprise us. It turns out, however, that she does care, and after biding her time for twelve years she sees to it that his death is avenged. We understand at last the meaning of the prophetic dream she had as a girl about her third marriage:

I seemed to have a gold bracelet on . . . but it did not seem as though this costly bracelet suited me that much better, though it was made of gold, not silver. Then I seemed to stumble and wanted to catch myself with my hand, but the gold bracelet struck against some stone and broke in two and blood seemed to ooze from the pieces. What I felt then seemed to me more like grief than loss, and it occurred to me that there had been a slight crack in the bracelet and when I looked at the pieces afterwards then I seemed to see many flaws in them. But yet I had the feeling that it might have remained whole had I guarded it better.

She had in fact cared for Bolli much more than she realized till after his death.

There is one more surprise for us. She takes a fourth husband, Thorkel, and the saga says: 'Thorkel and Gudrun came to love each other very much', the identical phrase that was used to describe the marriage of Kjartan and

72

Hrefna. Yet, for all this, she remains a romantic heroine. When she is very old and pious, her son by Bolli asks her whom she had loved the most.

> Thorkel, she said, was the mightiest and the greatest chieftain, but no man was more accomplished or capable than Bolli. Thord was the wisest of them and the greatest lawspeaker. Thorgald I'll not even count. Then Bolli Bollasson said: I plainly see from what you are telling me how it was with each of your husbands, but it still remains unsaid which man you loved the most. There is no need for you to hide this any longer now. Gudrun said: You are pressing me hard, my son, but if I must tell this to anyone, then I would rather have it be you. To him I was worst whom I loved most. I think, said Bollasson, that the truth has now been told.

The primary world contemporary with the writers of the saga is not the world they describe. By their time the attempt to create a rural democracy had failed. The family blood feuds over matters of personal honour had degenerated into ruthless power politics, a general state of anarchy which ended in the loss of independence; in 1262 Iceland became a province of the Norwegian Crown. If as Historians they try to depict the past as objectively as possible, as Poets this past has the attractions of a secondary world, nobler and more intelligible than the present in which they are living, and it is precisely because the characters from that time be numinous to their imaginations that the writers feel it their duty to narrate their stories as truthfully as possible; heroes deserve nothing less.

The marriage in each of us, whether as writers or readers, between the Historian and the Poet first began to run into serious difficulties in the seventeenth century, but it is only in the industrialized societies of the last hundred and fifty years that, by the time most of us are twenty, the two have divorced.

The consequences are only too obvious. The primary world, as perceived by the divorced Historian, is a de-sacralized, depersonalized world where all facts are equally profane. Human history becomes a matter of statistics, in which individual human beings are represented as faceless and anonymous puppets of impersonal forces. The charac-teristic virtue of the Historian, his impartiality, which refrains from intruding his own moral values upon events, leaving that duty to the reader, becomes meaningless, for moral judgements can be passed only on personal deeds, and in the world he depicts men are incapable of deeds and exhibit only social behaviour.

The divorced Poet, on the other hand, can find materials for building his secondary worlds only in his private subjectivity. His characteristic virtue, a sense of the sacred, the personal, becomes concentrated upon himself. The narcissism which is right and proper to every individual – for no one can or should think of himself as profane, an impersonal puppet of fate, but as a child of God – turns into self-idolatry. He and he alone *is* God; all others are things.

In modern art one feels that the artist is demanding, first, that we shall admire what he has made, not on its objective merits but because it is his (it must be good because he made it) and, second, that we shall devote the whole of our lives to a study of his works and ignore all others.

If he does attempt to deal with the primary world, something even nastier is apt to result. If, as the Historian says, all facts are equally profane, he cannot deal with it at all; in order to deal with it, his imagination turns to what one can only call devil worship; that is to say, he attaches sacred importance to, and only to, what in the primal world is base, horrible, evil. It is necessary that we know about the evil in the world – about past evil that we may know what man is capable of and be on the watch for it in ourselves, and about present evil so that we may take

74

political action to eradicate it. This knowledge it is one of the duties of the Historian to impart. But the Poet cannot get into this business without defiling himself and his audience. To write a play (that is, to construct a secondary world) about Auschwitz, for example, is wicked; author and audience may try to pretend that they are morally horrified, but in fact they are passing an entertaining evening together in the aesthetic enjoyment of horrors.

There are certain art forms which, by their intrinsic nature, are defended against this kind of decadence and can therefore continue to exist only so long as people exist to whom the concepts of the sacred, the heroic, freedom, personal freedom and responsibility have real meaning. One of these is opera, and to opera I shall devote my next lecture.

III

THE WORLD OF OPERA

In the primary world, we all have experienced occasions when, as we say, we felt like singing. We may sometimes even attempt to sing, but if we do, we are dissatisfied with the results for two reasons. First, most of us cannot produce pleasing sounds; second, even if we are professional singers, we cannot compose a song expressly for the occasion but can only sing some song that already is in existence, which we happen to know; in the hypothetical case of someone who was both a singer and a composer, he would be equally baffled because music takes time to compose, and by the time he had composed something for the occasion, the occasion would be over. However, an examination of the kinds of situation and experience in the primary world which make us feel like singing offer a clue to the kind of secondary world which opera can create.

There are always extraordinary situations or states of violent emotion in which we feel an urgent need for utterance – we cannot remain silent – and feel that words would be an inadequate medium for such utterance. Why we should feel that song would be adequate where words are not is a difficult question to answer. I think it has something to do with the fact that our use of words is by no means confined to formalized literary forms like poetry and fiction, that words are our medium for everyday informal communication with other members of our own species concerning practical affairs and that, in the primary world, most of our normal conversation is addressed to or elicited by another individual and thought of as private, that is to say, as concerning the speaker and the listener only, not an audience. That is why, when we watch a play which attempts to portray everyday social life realistically, we feel in the position of peeping Toms, spying on the actors who are playing to each other, unaware that they are being watched and overheard. It is an essential aspect of the art of realistic acting that the actor should never seem to notice the audience. Consequently, when we speak, however passionately, we cannot forget our use of words for banal and profane purposes. Furthermore, when our emotional state passes a certain degree of intensity, even when, as in love, another human being seems to be its cause, it seems to be of universal significance. It is no longer sufficient that the girl we love shall know that we love her; the whole world must know.

The formalized art of poetry goes some way to meet our needs – a verse drama already involves the audience as well as the protagonists – but music goes much further.

For singing is a form of public outcry: it is on the voluntary level what an *ouch* of pain or the howl of a hungry baby is on the involuntary.

It is possible to speak in two manners, in prose or in verse. But there are no two ways of singing; the only alternative to song is silence. Though few have the talent for composing verses, almost anybody can be taught to speak them at least adequately. Anybody, one is tempted to say, except professional actors. Trained to manage the naturalistic prose dialogue which most modern dramas call for, the average modern actor is terrified of verse and does everything he can, by ignoring the line endings and excessive rubato, to make it sound as much like naturalistic prose as possible. While it is equally the case that few have the talent for composing vocal music, very few can be taught to sing. To possess the vocal chords which can make sounds which other people want to listen to is a gift granted to very few. Singing, like classical ballet dancing, is a virtuoso art. A virtuoso art can be tragic or comic, but it has only one style, the high style; a low or humble style and virtuosity are incompatible. If one listens to a recording of an opera, written and sung in a language one does not know, one can recognize the particular emotional state, love, rage, grief or joy, which the singer is expressing at any given momemt, but one cannot tell whether the singer is a duchess or a chambermaid, a prince or a policeman: song, that is to say, abolishes all social and age differences. Indeed, in some operas, like *Rosenkavalier* and *Arabella*, one cannot even identify the singer's sex. Nor, I think, can one tell, from the evidence of one's ears alone, whether the singer be a noble hero or a wicked villain.

When one can guess, it is because the composer is obeying certain historical conventions. By convention, for example, the noble hero is a tenor, the wicked villain a *baritono cattivo*, old men are basses, and the voices of servants have a lighter timbre than that of their masters or mistresses. But this is purely a convention which a composer is free to ignore if he wishes.

There can be, therefore, no such thing as a *verismo* opera. The so-called *verismo* operas are simply dramas in which exotic settings and characters have replaced the gods and courtesans, gypsies, bohemians, princes, etc., of the Courtly Baroque; both are equally secondary worlds very far removed from the primary world of our everyday experience.

The job of the librettist is to furnish the composer with a plot, characters and words: of these, the least important, so far as the audience is concerned, are the words. The opera house is not a *Lieder* recital hall, and they will be very fortunate if they hear one word in seven. The verbal text of an opera is to be judged not by the literary quality or lack of it which it may have when read but by its success or failure in exciting the musical imagination of the composer. This does not mean that its literary quality is of no importance. Most composers will be more stimulated by good verses than silly ones, provided that they are so written as to be settable to musical notes and singable. Would it not be better, one may ask at this point, if all composers wrote their own libretti, like Wagner? If most do not, the reason is not, I think, merely that they feel incompetent to write one. However much preliminary discussion may have gone on between composer and librettist, the former cannot know what the actual text will be till he receives it; when he does, it will present him with problems he has not foreseen, and the challenge of solving these is a stimulus to his imagination, which would be lacking if he had written the text himself.

Verbal speech and music are two kinds of language, and if they are to be married successfully, it is essential to know in what ways they differ from each other, and what are the virtues and limitations of each. A verbal statement and a musical phrase are both a temporal succession of sounds that take time to say or to play. But words, unlike notes, have denotative meanings; consequently, in most verbal statements there is no relation between the temporal succession of the words and the thought which they express. In a narrative statement, like 'I turned the corner and saw a raven', there is a little, but even here my act of seeing and the raven I see are one event, not two, and in a statement like 'Jones is six feet tall', time does not enter into its meaning at all. In music there is no such conflict; only pure succession. When we speak, that is to say, usually we are 'stopping to think'. But music is always going on to become.

In verbal speech one can say, 'I love you'. Music can, I believe, express the equivalent of 'I love', but it is incapable of saying whom or what I love, you, God or the decimal system. In this respect it is at the opposite pole to the language of painting. A painting can portray someone as beautiful, lovable, etc., but it cannot say who, if anybody, loves this person. Music, one might say, is always intransitive and in the first person; painting has only one voice, the passive, and only the third person singular or plural.

Both of them also have only the present indicative tense and no negative. For this reason, it makes no sense to ask of a piece of music or a painting: does the composer or the painter mean what he says, or is he just pretending? Lying or self-deception can be expressed by neither. Verbal speech, on the other hand, has three persons, singular and plural, past, present and future tenses, an active and a passive voice, but in a certain sense one might say that most verbal statements are in the subjunctive mood, that is to say, verifiable, if at all, by appeal to non-verbal facts.

This being so, what elements in verbal speech can most readily be wedded to musical notes to produce song? To begin with, obviously, the more dynamic verbal elements, interjections, like 'oh', 'alas', 'hail', verbs of motion like running, flying, swimming, verbs indicating the physical concomitants of emotion, like laughing, weeping, sighing, and phrases expressing temporal succession or repetition. Rossini once said: 'Give me a laundry list, and I will set it.' He may have intended to say that the artistic quality of the words was of no consequence to him, but in fact any list is eminently suitable to musical setting, as are, because of the essentially public nature of music, all nouns which denote beings or emotions, concepts which are universally felt, consciously or unconsciously, to be of sacral importance: the sun, the moon, the sea, the four elements, god, death, grief, love, joy, etc.

To be avoided by a librettist as difficult or impossible to set, are first, puns or double meanings. For instance, the line 'Farewell, thou art too dear for my possessing' is unsettable, because there is no musical way of conveying the two meanings of *dear* as *precious* and *expensive*. Verse which relies for its effect on its visual imagery or upon complicated metaphors is also unsuitable: music cannot imitate visual facts, and a complicated metaphor like 'the crowd that spanielled him at heel' takes more time to grasp than music can give it, even if, as is unlikely, the audience can hear every word.

Then it seems to be an empirical fact – I suspect it has something to do with musical tempi being generally slower than speech tempi – that composers find short lines of verse easier to set than long ones. The decasyllabic line of English blank verse and heroic couplet, for example, appears to be too long for natural musical phrases.

The question which a librettist must continually ask himself is: can I imagine this line I have just written gaining in emotional impact if it is sung instead of being spoken? If he cannot, then the chances are that his composer will feel the same. It is possible to write a verbal opera. The purest example in English literature that I know of is *The Importance of Being Earnest*, a play in which every other dramatic element is subordinated to the dialogue: the characters have no existence apart from what they say; the sole purpose of the plot is to give them opportunities to make their remarks; and the dramatic effect of *what* they say is inseparable from how they say it, from the cadence and rhythms of the spoken voice. For this reason one has only to attend a performance of Wilde's comedy to know that the greatest composer on earth could have nothing to add to it.

When writing an aria or an ensemble Mr Kallman and I found it helpful to let our choice of words and style be guided by a Platonic idea of a suitable melody. Naturally, we were not such fools as to breathe a word about this but, to our utmost astonishment and delight every time, both Stravinsky and Henze composed actual music that corresponded to our Platonic ideas.

CHARACTERS

Since Mozart's time the librettist has been expected to

provide the composer with characters who are interesting as well as capable of singing. Most eighteenth-century *opera seria* before Mozart deserves the epithet 'canary fodder', which has been unjustly applied to the operas of Bellini and Donizetti, for in it one operatic element, virtuoso singing, was exalted to the almost total neglect of character and plot interest. A typical opera of this kind consisted of a succession of elaborate *da capo* arias, preceded by short passages of recitative, an occasional duet but no ensemble, and after each aria the singer left the stage. All that the librettist was expected to do was to provide a few lines of singable verse, expressing stereotyped emotions and moral judgements, the words of which could be repeated as often as the composer's musical ideas required. In consequence, very few operas of the period have remained viable as stage works, however beautiful some of their music. Mozart broke through the convention with his extended and symphonically treated finales. Bellini and Donizetti realized the great dramatic possibilities of the ensemble. And in different ways Verdi and Wagner broke away from the formal symmetrical aria and at the same time gave the recitative dramatic and lyrical qualities which it had previously lacked. If we use the term 'music drama' in a less specialized sense than Wagner, one may say that every successful opera since Mozart has been a music drama.

Because of the dynamic nature of music and the virtuoso nature of singing, opera cannot deal successfully with passive characters or helpless victims of fate. To sing is the most gratuitous of acts, so that the world of opera is a world of personal deeds: nothing can happen in it which a psychologist could term socially conditioned behaviour. The characters best suited to inhabit it are not only passionate but wilfully so, persons who insist upon their fate, however tragically dreadful or comically absurd. In opera a sorrowing character must never actually weep; he must sing his grief, that is to say, remain its master. On the other hand, provided his characters are wilful, the librettist can take them from any class he pleases; he can even, as Janáček's admirable opera *The Cunning Little Vixen* demonstrates, include animals in his cast.

A secondary world must draw its building materials from the primary world, but it can only take such material as its creator is capable of imaginatively recombining and transforming. In practice, this seems to mean that no secondary world can have a setting in the immediate present. The factuality of the present is too strong to imagine as other than it is, too strong, at least, if the present situation involves strong emotions and suffering; it may be possible to write an *opera buffa* with a contemporary setting but not an *opera seria*. The apparent exceptions, *Cav* and *Pag*, for example, were acceptable when they were first produced only because the opera-going public at the beginning of this century was not composed of Sicilian peasants or travelling actors. In a class-stratified society the various classes are only apparently contemporaneous, for they inhabit different primary worlds.

At the same time no secondary world can fully hold our attention unless it has something significant to say – we need not necessarily be consciously aware of what it is – about our present life. The most successful heroes and heroines in opera are mythical figures, that is to say, whatever their historical and geographical setting, they embody some element of human nature, some aspect of the human condition which is of permanent concern to human beings irrespective of their time and place. Perhaps I should modify this and say that while no genuine myth is ever totally irrelevant, their rank of importance varies with time and place. To one age or one culture *this* myth may seem more relevant, to another age and culture *that* one. Further, historical and cultural changes may produce new myths. Kafka was not only a genius but also a twentieth-century one.

Nietzsche showed great insight when he wrote of Wagner's libretti:

> Would you believe it, that Wagner's heroines one and all, once they have been divested of their heroic husks, are almost undistinguishable from Madame Bovary, just as one can conceive conversely of Flaubert being well able to transform all his heroines into Scandinavian or Carthaginian women, and then offer them to Wagner in their mythologized form as a libretto? Indeed, generally speaking, Wagner does not seem to have become interested in any problems other than those which engross the little Parisian decadents today, always five paces away from the hospital. All very modern problems, all problems which are at home in big cities.

Where Nietzsche was wrong was in imagining that this was a fault. Had Wagner been unable to feel in Norse mythology and the Niebelungen legends any relevance to the moral and social problems of the nineteenth century, he could not have made them come alive in his operas.

PLOT

Opera, said Goethe, is a succession of significant situations arranged in an artificial sequence. A good opera plot is one which provides as many and as varied situations in which it seems plausible that the characters should sing. This means that no opera plot can be sensible, for in sensible situations people do not sing; an opera plot must be, in both senses of the word, a melodrama. When sensible or unemotional moments occur in the story – and it is very difficult to eliminate them entirely – then the characters must either speak or employ a musical convention, like *recitativo secco*.

Of course, in a tragic opera, as in a spoken tragedy, a plausible situation, act and motive is to be preferred to an implausible, but music can make things credible or at least acceptable which in a spoken play would cause laughter. In a spoken play, for example, I think we should laugh if we were told that a woman had been careless enough to throw her own baby into the fire instead of the child of her enemy, but when this happens in *Il Trovatore* we have little difficulty in swallowing it. Again, the emotional persuasiveness of music is so much greater than that of words that a character in opera can switch from one state of feeling to another with an abruptness which in a spoken drama would be incredible. In the first act of Smetana's *Dalibor*, for instance, the heroine, Milada, enters and asks the King for vengeance upon Dalibor, who has just killed her brother. Dalibor is brought before the King and tells his life story. On hearing this, Milada falls in love with him immediately. As soon as he is led off to life imprisonment, she pleads with the King for mercy; her appeal fails, and the act ends with her planning to rescue him from his dungeon. As a spectator, I feel that the librettist should have been able to devise something more plausible but that, though in this act the libretto is weak, the weakness is not a fatal one. On the other hand, it is more difficult for the librettist than for the writer of spoken drama to convey a sense of dramatic movement. To sing something takes much longer than to say it, and when characters sing they must stand fairly still or they will not be heard, so that an opera is always in danger of turning into a static oratorio. When one examines the libretti of operas which succeed as dramatic stage works, one finds that the exits and entrances of the characters have a much greater significance than they have in spoken drama. An excellent example is the first act of *Tristan*. The act lasts one and a half hours, and the only actual event in it is the mutual drinking of the love potion by Tristan and Isolde, yet never does the act become static, and this is in large measure due to Wagner's extraordinary skill in handling and timing the entrances, exits and re-entrances of his four principal characters.

85

I shall devote the rest of this lecture to a description of the problems which Mr Chester Kallman and I encountered when working on the three libretti we have written together, *The Rake's Progress* for Igor Stravinsky, *Elegy for Young Lovers* and *The Bassarids*, both for Hans Werner Henze.

THE RAKE'S PROGRESS

In this case, it was Stravinsky who chose the subject. On looking at the Hogarth engravings, he had noticed that in the one depicting Bedlam there was a blind beggar playing a one-stringed fiddle, and this had excited his imagination. In the opera he actually wrote there is no such figure, but, as a sidelight on how a creative mind works, the anecdote has interest, I think.

Before starting work, it is essential that the librettist should know the style and scale of opera the composer has in mind. Stravinsky wished to write an opera of the Mozart kind, with set numbers, orchestral recitative and *recitativo secco* and an orchestra of a modest Mozartian size. This suited us fine, since for a beginner it is technically easier to write a libretto for such conventions than a music drama of the Wagnerian type. About the subject we felt less happy.

In his engravings Hogarth is not interested in the Rake as a person; his main concern is to make a series of pictures satirizing various aspects of life in eighteenth-century London. The only function of the Rake is to give the series a certain unity by appearing in them all. As he moves from one engraving to another, the previous figures he has been shown among disappear and he is seen in entirely new company. As a person, therefore, he has no history, for his relations to others are momentary and accidental. Further, the nature of the visual arts is such that they cannot portray inner conflict. Hogarth's Rake is a purely passive figure, whose role is to succumb to whatever temptation – lust, boredom, money, etc. – he is led into next. This filled us with dismay for, as I have said, passive characters cannot sing. So far as a story was concerned, all we had to start with was the basic premise of a young man who inherits a fortune, is corrupted by it and ends in penury and madness, and of the scenes in the series, only two, the Brothel and Bedlam, seemed obviously usable.

Our first problem, therefore, was to invent a history for our hero, to give him ties to a limited number of other characters, male and female, that should be both permanent and interesting. Secondly, though he would have to be shown as always yielding to temptation, he must also be shown as making some effort to resist, and the temptations should be of significantly different kinds. If he was to have any mythical resonance, though setting, costumes and diction might be eighteenth-century, he would have to be an embodiment of Everyman and the libretto a mixture of fairy-story and mediaeval morality play. If his moral conflicts were to be manifested on stage, we would require two characters, one who tempts and one who is tempted; as Faust is accompanied by Mephisto, we gave Tom Rakewell a servant, Nick Shadow. Tom does not, like Faust, know the identity of Nick from the beginning. On engaging Nick, Tom asks him what wages he wants; Nick replies evasively, saying that he will tell him when a year and a day have passed. Tom agrees to this, and, of course, when the time is up, Nick Shadow reveals himself as the Devil and asks for his soul. Now we had at least continuous roles for two singers.

As a compensation, not altogether satisfactory, for Tom's passivity, we decided to make him a manic-depressive, at one moment up in the clouds, at the next down in the dumps; this would, at least, give his role some musical variety. As a structural device we used one so common in fairy-tales, that of the three wishes. Tom's are: 'I wish I had money', 'I wish I were happy', 'I wish it were true'.

Each time he makes a wish Nick Shadow immediately appears, the first time to tell him that an uncle has left him a fortune, the second time to suggest a fantastic marriage and the third time with a bogus machine for turning stones into bread about which Tom has just been dreaming. Finally when, thanks to a girl's semi-divine intervention, he wins a card game with Shadow and so saves his soul, though not his sanity, he cries: 'I wish for nothing else.'

Of the three roles for female voices we thought up, one was easy and obvious but minor, since she could appear in only one scene, Mother Goose, the Madam of a brothel. As a counter to Nick Shadow we provided our hero with a guardian angel, Anne Truelove, to whom he is engaged when the opera begins and whose image he cherishes in his heart through all his debaucheries and follies. She, for her part, loves him for better or worse and in the end saves him from damnation. It must be frankly admitted that, though Stravinsky has given her very beautiful music to sing, she cannot be called a character of much interest; she is just a very good girl indeed with a fine soprano voice. For this defect we are, of course, responsible, but I doubt if, given the subject, another librettist could have done much better.

Our other major female role is, we think, more interesting: at least she profoundly shocked some of the critics. In one of the Hogarth engravings, the Rake marries an ugly old heiress for her money, but we had already shown Tom succumbing to the temptations of wealth. We decided, therefore, to be fashionably modern, and make him, at Shadow's suggestion, commit an *acte gratuite*. In order to assert his freedom of will from the compulsions of Passion and Reason, he marries Baba the Turk, a lady from the circus with a magnificent Assyrian beard. To read into this, as some critics did, obscene sexual innuendos, can only be done by ignoring both the text and the music. It is true that the part calls for careful playing; it must on no account be played for laughs. In her own eyes, Baba is as much a *grande dame* as the Marschallin in *Rosenkavalier*, immensely proud of her beard as a visible sign of her genius, that which gives her a high status in her circus world.

ELEGY FOR YOUNG LOVERS

Henze came to us and said that he wished to write an opera which, though intended for performance in ordinary opera houses, would be a chamber opera in the sense that it would be concerned with a small number of strongly differentiated but closely related characters, with no chorus and, if possible, only one set. A possible subject, he thought, might be a Pirandello-like one: Each character might have his or her particular delusion or obsession, and the dramatic interest would come from their mutual misunderstanding of each other. This request seemed to us a challenge. From a spoken play we demand complexity of character, subtlety of motivation and interesting dialogue. Just how far could one go in writing a libretto which should exhibit these qualities but still remain a libretto that demanded to be set to music and sung? Also, how near to the present time could we make the setting and still create an acceptable secondary world?

The location, we decided, should be a *Gasthaus* in the Austrian Alps some years before the First World War. Later than that would be too risky. Casting about for possible characters, those we at first came up with were as follows:

1. a lady's maid on her holiday, masquerading as a great lady; this she is able to do convincingly because, as a person, she has all the instincts of an aristocrat and it is only an accident of birth that she is not one;
2. a young man, probably a born aristocrat, who would fall in love with her. Since the opera was not to be a satirical comedy, she must not suffer the comic exposure.

That is to say, she must die before her lover discovers she is not what she pretends to be. This seemed to require that she be already suffering from some fatal disease, which would require —

3. a doctor in whom she confides;
4. a Miss Haversham sort of character, a widow whose husband fell into a crevasse on their honeymoon, from which his body has never emerged. For years she has lived in the inn, believing that one day he will return;
5. an elderly actor whose great ambition in life is to play the lead in Byron's *Manfred*, has come to the inn to get atmosphere and, indeed, has come to believe that he *is* Manfred.

At this point we got utterly stuck. We had, in fact, no myth. After days of complete frustration, we realized that the principal character must be the older man, though he could not be an actor. What kind of person, we asked ourselves, could be simultaneously and for good reasons related to a young girl, a doctor and a crazy old widow? Suddenly we got the answer. A great Poet.

Now we had our mythical figure. As I have said, now and again a new myth appears, and the European Romantics created the myth of the Artistic Genius. If, as they believed, the supreme human achievement is to make a great work of art, then the artist is the most god-like of human beings and deserves the semi-divine honours paid in earlier times to the Epic Hero. Further, if it should prove necessary in order to create a masterpiece, the artist must be prepared ruthlessly to sacrifice his own life and happiness and those of others. He is not to be judged by the moral standards we apply to ordinary mortals.

What had prevented us from coming to this conclusion earlier was, I fancy, that we had been thinking too much in terms of spoken drama. In a spoken drama an artist cannot be portrayed, since it is not his appearance or his social actions that make a man a great poet but the poetry he writes. All that Shaw can do with Marchbanks, the poet in *Candida*, is endow him with the artistic temperament, a disease which, as Chesterton said, afflicts only amateurs. Even had Shaw been a great poet himself, he could only have written Shavian poetry, not a different but equally great kind of poetry which the audience would believe had been written by Marchbanks. But in an opera, it seemed to us, it might be possible to portray a poet convincingly because poetry and music are different kinds of language. If, at certain moments, the poetry of our hero could be represented by music, the audience would, if the music were good enough, be convinced that his poetry was good, although, as a matter of fact, the music was written not by him but by Henze. The function of the plot would then be to show the relation between the secondary worlds of the poems written by our hero and his experiences as a man in the primary world.

Once we knew who our hero was, it was easy to decide on the other characters and even on the kind of voices their roles would require.

Gregor Mittenhofer *(baritone)*, a famous poet, now nearing sixty, began life as a postman, was discovered by Carolina, Gräfin von Kirchstetten *(contralto)*, and enabled, thanks to her financial patronage, to devote all his time to poetry. In addition, by acting as his secretary and housekeeper, Carolina relieves him of all practical chores. For the past ten years another admirer, Dr Wilhelm Reischmann *(bass)*, who is a widower, has kept him in good health and youthful vigour with medicines and hormone injections. Their attitude towards him is a mixture of admiration, amusement and possessiveness: he is their big baby, who could not manage without them. Lately he has acquired as a mistress another young admirer Elizabeth Zimmer *(soprano)*, of whom, as might be expected, Carolina is suspicious and resentful. A permanent resident of the Black Eagle Inn, where the four of them now are, is Frau Hilda Mack *(coloratura soprano)*, our Miss Haversham

91

character, who from time to time goes into trances and has visions. Remembering that Yeats had a wife from whose mediumistic gifts he profited, it seemed plausible that Mittenhofer should have discovered Frau Mack and made it his habit to visit her from time to time, bringing his entourage with him.

ACT I

Doctor Reischmann is expecting the arrival of his son, and Mittenhofer's godson, Toni *(tenor)*. Mittenhofer is in a very bad temper because he has been at the inn for over a week but Frau Mack has not yet obliged with a vision. Toni, who is at an age when most young men feel critically hostile to their elders, arrives and Mittenhofer introduces him to Elizabeth. As they shake hands, Frau Mack goes into a trance. They withdraw, leaving Mittenhofer alone with her, taking notes of what she says. As he hoped, her vision gives him the first inklings for a new poem, not the poem itself or even its theme, but a certain tone of voice, some key images and hints as to its form. Now he will be able to start working again. Then something unexpected happens. A mountain guide, Josef Mauer *(a spoken role)*, enters to announce that the body of Frau Mack's husband has emerged from the glacier, forty years after he fell into a crevasse. Elizabeth is entrusted with the task of breaking the news to her. Frau Mack is dazed at first but the years of timeless waiting are over and she will have to change her life.

ACT II (Some days later)

Toni and Elizabeth have fallen in love with each other, or imagine they have. Their love duet and embrace is interrupted by a horrified Carolina. When she informs Mittenhofer, he tells her that he already knows but does not take their affair seriously. Though the ultimate consequence for them is to be tragic, in a sense he is right. For the past few days Elizabeth has been shocked and antagonized by

Mittenhofer's strange behaviour towards Frau Mack. The discovery of her husband's body has transformed her. She has exchanged the 1870 dresses she has worn for forty years for the latest fashions of 1910, started to smoke and drink and spends most of her time playing cards with the mountain guides. More seriously for Mittenhofer, she has announced that she is never going to have another trance again, so that he has been deprived of a valued source of inspiration, and he has taken this very badly. In this mood of antagonism Elizabeth has been drawn to Toni, who can share it, and persuaded herself that, after all, it is more natural for a girl to fall in love with a boy of her own age than with an older man. In actual fact, though at the moment she is feeling hostile towards him, she is more physically attracted by Mittenhofer than by Toni. For Toni, by temperament introverted and shy, she is the first girl who has shown any interest in him: he is not really in love with her but in love with the idea of being in love. If their affair had remained clandestine, it is probable that they would both have realized this and, when his holiday was over, it would have died a natural death. Mittenhofer has seen what the situation is and therefore kept his knowledge to himself. But the moment the affair becomes publicly known, Elizabeth is compelled to make a choice between Mittenhofer and Toni. For the young pair, too, the violent disapproval of Carolina and Toni's father is an affront to their pride, which makes any calm assessment of their feelings impossible.

After a long interview with Mittenhofer, in which he first disarms her by showing her that he knows very well just how selfish and childish he is and then, in his account of what it is like to be a poet whose life is subordinate to his work, cunningly appeals to her compassion, Elizabeth decides that she cannot leave him and tells Toni so. A scene follows, interrupted by the entrance of Frau Mack in high spirits and slightly tipsy, in which everybody except Mittenhofer becomes hysterical. Unable to bear all the others shouting at her, in a gesture of defiance Elizabeth asks Toni to marry her. Frau Mack warns her that she is making a mistake, that what she should do is leave both Mittenhofer and Toni and come back with her to Vienna. Mittenhofer, on the other hand, appears to approve and, to calm everyone down, says he will tell them something about the new poem he has been working on for which he now has a title, *The Young Lovers*. In the sextet that follows the others react to his description of the poem in terms of their present emotions, and the very beautiful music which Henze has written for it will convince any audience, I believe, that the poem is going to be a very good one. After the sextet is over, Mittenhofer says he has one last request to make of Elizabeth and Toni before they go off together. Now that Frau Mack has failed him, he must fall back on another imaginative stimulus which he has found effective in the past, namely to sleep with a sprig of *edelweiss* beneath his pillow. As a gesture of reconciliation and goodwill, will they, for his sake, stay one more day and ascend the Hammerhorn to gather him some? To this they gladly agree. Mittenhofer asks to be left alone. His assumed calm and good temper vanish and he explodes with rage against the whole lot of them, Toni, Elizabeth, Carolina, the Doctor, Frau Mack. 'Why don't they all die?' he bellows.

ACT III

Toni and Elizabeth have left to climb the Hammerhorn. Doctor Reischmann and Frau Mack are all packed, ready to return to Vienna. Upstairs, through the open door of his study, Mittenhofer is heard trying out rhymes for his poem. Farewells are said, and Mittenhofer and Carolina are left alone together, which is what she has always wished for. 'I must get back to work,' he says, 'and try to finish my *Elegy* in time for my sixtieth birthday.' 'Elegy? What Elegy?' she asks. 'The poem, the poem,' he replies. Carolina then asks him why he not only let Elizabeth leave him for Toni but even seemed to approve of and desire it. 'The atmosphere had become impossible,' he says. 'As for the young lovers, what will happen to them? Will it last a year? I doubt it. And then, what will they do?' Mauer, the guide, enters to say that a severe storm is brewing in the mountains and anyone caught in it will be in grave danger. There is just time, however, if they leave at once, for experienced mountaineers to bring such persons back to safety. Has anyone from the inn gone there? Slowly and deliberately, Mittenhofer says: 'Nobody that I know of.' Carolina stifles a cry, and Mauer leaves. In the scene that follows, Carolina starts to go mad. Mittenhofer's murderous lie, though the law cannot touch him, will not go unpunished. He will never be able to get rid of Carolina but for the rest of his life must live with someone who knows what he has done. The scene changes to the Hammerhorn where, in the face of the imminent reality of death, Toni and Elizabeth realize, without reproaching each other, that their love has been an illusion. This scene, for which, incidentally, I was responsible, will not do at all and must some day be completely rewritten. To my fond eye it reads well and might be effective in a spoken verse play. But for opera it is far too literary and complicated in the argument, far too dependent upon every word being heard, to get across when set to music.

EPILOGUE

Mittenhofer appears before the curtain in tails and says in a speaking voice:

Your Serene Highness, Your Excellency, the Minister of Culture, Ladies and Gentlemen. I am going to open my reading with the last poem I have written, *Elegy for Young Lovers*. It is dedicated to the memory of Toni Reischmann and Elizabeth Zimmer, a beautiful and very brave couple, who, as some of you know, recently perished on the Hammerhorn. 'In death they were not divided.'

He proceeds to read the poem, but what we hear is not words but music from the orchestra and vocalized sounds from behind the curtain sung by all the other characters who have, in one way or another, helped him to write it.

THE BASSARIDS

A number of years back Mr Kallman and I told Mr Henze that we thought the *Bacchae* of Euripides was excellent potential material for a grand opera libretto, since the myth seemed to us exceptionally relevant to our own day.

The eighteenth century took it for granted that, in a conflict between Reason and Unreason, Reason was bound in the end to be victorious. So in *Die Zauberflöte* the Queen of the Night has a daughter, Pamina; Sarastro acquires a princely disciple, Tamino; the two young innocents fall in love, and the curtain falls upon preparations for their wedding. Even a century later a librettist or a composer, looking for a suitable operatic subject, would probably have rejected the *Bacchae* as too unnatural. Such events, they would have said, may have occurred in a primitive barbaric society, but social and intellectual progress have made it impossible for anything of the kind ever to occur again. For the nineteenth century the myth was moribund.

Today we know only too well that it is as possible for whole communities to become demonically possessed as it is for individuals to go off their heads. Further, what the psychologists have taught us about repression and its damaging, sometimes fatal, effects makes us look at Sarastro with a more critical eye. Like Pentheus when confronted by the cult of Dionysus, Sarastro's only idea of how to deal with the Queen of the Night is to use force, magical in his case, and banish her to the Underworld. 'Suppose', we cannot help wondering, 'there had been no Tamino and Pamina to provide a tidy and happy ending, would Sarastro have enjoyed his triumph for long? Is it not more likely that, in the end, he would have suffered at the hands of the implacable Queen as horrid a fate as Pentheus?'

In the case of *The Rake's Progress* we had given us an outline of a story but no characters; in the case of *Elegy for Young Lovers* we had neither a story nor characters; but in the case of *The Bassarids*, Euripides had provided us with both.

Certain scenes in his tragedy, notably the scene in which Pentheus confronts the disguised Dionysus, the scene in which Dionysus hypnotizes Pentheus till he is willing to dress up as a woman and go to Mount Cytheron and the scene in which Cadmus brings Agave out of her trance to a realization of the appalling thing she has done, seemed to us excellent operatic material as they stood, so that our libretto could in these scenes follow the original text pretty closely.

Elsewhere, however, a good many changes would have to be made.

In the *Bacchae*, the only important solo roles are those of Dionysus and Pentheus, both male. Agave does not appear until the play is almost over. Euripides assigns the most important role of all to a female chorus. At first sight, this might seem admirably suited to an opera, but, in fact, this is not so. We know that the chorus in Greek tragedy both chanted and danced, though we know almost nothing about classical Greek music and choreography. Today vocal choral writing and ballet choreography demand so much more technical skill from performers that it is now an axiom that singers cannot dance and dancers cannot sing. Furthermore, though nineteenth-century composers often introduced ballets into their operas, to introduce one today would be asking for trouble, since no opera house can now afford a first-rate ballet company: at a contemporary performance of *La Gioconda*, for example, the spectacle of the Dance of the Hours usually makes one squirm with embarrassment. But if an opera is to be a dramatic stage work, not static oratorio, then a non-dancing chorus must be used very sparingly. Accordingly, we found that we had to transfer much that Euripides gives the chorus to say to the soloists, and we changed the chorus of women only to a mixed chorus. The *Bacchae* opens with a speech by Dionysus to the audience, in which he tells them that he has already filled Agave and her sisters with madness as a punishment for denying his divinity so that they have run off to Mount Cytheron and goes on to tell the audience what is going to happen to Pentheus. After his speech Pentheus, who has, it would seem, been King of Thebes for some time, returns from a journey and learns for the first time of the Dionysian cult. It seemed to us that in an opera what Dionysus narrates should be presented in dramatic action. When *The Bassarids* begins, therefore, Cadmus has just abdicated in favour of his grandson. The Dionysian cult is already popular in Thebes, but Agave has not yet succumbed to it. Pentheus' first act as King is to ban the cult.

To Euripides' cast we added three women characters. We gave Autonoe, Agave's sister (who, though she appears in the play, does not speak by herself) a solo role. In the Semele legend Semele had a servant, Beroe; in our libretto Agave took her on after Semele's death to act as nurse to the child Pentheus. And we introduced a handsome captain of the Royal Guard by whom Agave is attracted, though she is much too fastidious to have an affair with him. The conventions of Greek tragedy did not require Euripides to explain why Pentheus objected so strongly to the Dionysian cult, or why Cadmus and Tiresias approved; all he had to do was to describe the fatal *hubris* of Pentheus, a mortal, in opposing a god. But for a contemporary music drama, it seemed to us that we should make explicit and differentiate the religious attitudes of the various characters, all of which, we trust, would have been comprehensible to an audience in Euripides' time. Thus Cadmus, now very old, has become the victim of superstitious terrors. He has learned by bitter experience that the gods are not only powerful but also jealous competitors for men's worship. It is difficult to pay reverence to one without giving offence to another, and giving offence, however unintentionally, always brings misfortune. As he is unable to decide for himself whether Dionysus is or is not a god, the rise of his cult is one more occasion for dread. If Dionysus is divine and he, as King of Thebes, refuses to give the cult official sanction, divine vengeance will fall on the city. On the other hand, if Dionysus is only an ordinary mortal, sanction will outrage the existing gods. Rather than take a decision he has abdicated and left the responsibility to Pentheus. Euripides portrays Tiresias as a rather silly old man, whose legendary powers of prophecy are not in evidence. We have exaggerated the silliness and made him an old man whose fear of death takes the form of trying to keep up with the young. He is enthusiastic about the cult of Dionysus simply because it is new, the latest thing in religious fashion.

Agave has lost all faith in the traditional polytheism in which she was brought up and, when the opera opens, believes in nothing. She is lonely and unhappy, feelings she hides behind a mask of cynical bitchiness, though really a passionate nature. The obvious cause of her loneliness is that she has been left a widow when still fairly young, and there is no man of equal rank whom she could take as a second husband. Her dissatisfaction, however, goes much deeper than sexual frustration. Though not consciously aware of it, she is desperately looking for some faith which will give her life meaning and purpose. Such a faith Dionysus seems to offer.

Her first experience of the Dionysian ecstasy, about which she sings when brought back from Mount Cytheron, is entirely happy and harmless, a kind of Wordsworthian, pantheistic vision of nature.

One may suppose, if one likes, that Pentheus has visited Ionia and studied under one of the philosophers there. At any rate, he has discarded polytheism, the gods of which have all the passions and vices of mortals, and come to believe in the One Good, universal, impersonal, apprehensible to human reason. For him the source of blindness and evil is the flesh with its passions. As King of Thebes, he is willing to tolerate the traditional cults for the time being, but not the new cult of Dionysus, which seems to him the deliberate worship of irrational passion. His attempt to completely repress his own instinctual life instead of trying to integrate it with his rationality puts him into Dionysus' hands.

Beroe we imagined as being descended from a people who had once ruled Greece before it was conquered and enslaved by the Dorian invaders. She has remained faithful to the archaic cult of the Mother-Goddess and never accepted the male-dominated Olympus of her masters.

Our only substantial additions to the story as told by Euripides are a comic intermezzo and a new finale. In the early days of opera it was the custom to sandwich a one-act *opera buffa* between the two acts of an *opera seria*. Such a convention provided a musical and verbal contrast which both we and Henze felt would be desirable if it could be made an integral part of the opera. As in Euripides, our Pentheus falls under Dionysus' hypnotic spell and is intensely curious to learn what his mother and her fellow Bacchantes are actually doing on Mount Cytheron. Dionysus tells Beroe to bring Agave's mirror and makes Pentheus look into it. In the intermezzo which follows what the audience sees are Pentheus' fantasies of what they are doing, the fantasies of a sexually repressed man. Agave, Autonoe, Tiresias and the Captain of the Guard appear dressed like actors in some pastoral play at an eighteenth-century French court and act out a charade. Though, as is proper for an eighteenth-century setting, the Greek names have been romanized, the subject of the charade is another Greek myth, *The Judgement of Calliope*, a court trial in which the rival litigants, Venus, played by Agave, and Proserpine, played by Autonoe, each assert

their exclusive right to keep Adonis, played by the Captain,
as a lover. The verdict of the judge, Calliope, played by
Tiresias, is that he shall spend one third of the year with
each, and have the remaining third to himself as a respite
from their insatiable demands. The atmosphere of the
intermezzo is decadent, indecent in a giggly way, but not
in the least serious or dangerous. When it is over, Pentheus
sets off for Mount Cytheron to see for himself, and the
reality is, of course, both serious and mortally dangerous.

Euripides' tragedy ends with Dionysus banishing
Cadmus and Agave from Thebes. In our libretto Dionysus
now orders the Captain of the Guard to set fire to the
palace. The scrim descends and flames rise, completely
hiding the stage. From behind the scrim Dionysus is
heard summoning his mother, Semele, from the grave to
be apotheosized on Olympus as the Goddess Thyone. The
flames die down, and the scrim rises. The sky is of a
dazzling Mediterranean blue. Of the palace only a jagged,
blackened wall remains. Upon Semele's tomb stand two
enormous primitive fertility idols of an African or South
Seas type. The male is daubed with red paint. Visors
down, the Guard stand about the base of the tomb. In a
semicircle around it cluster the chorus, some kneeling,
some prostrate. A little girl, who in an earlier scene, and
together with her mother, had been put to the torture,
runs forward with a doll, which she smashes against the
base of the tomb and then stamps on.

Last, a word about the costumes. To dress all the characters in Greek costume would be risky, since it demands
the kind of figure which few opera singers possess. To live,
as we do, in an historically conscious age means that for
us each historical epoch has its typical character and
attitude to life, which are reflected in what it wears. It
seemed to us, therefore, that we could use clothing as a
kind of visual shorthand, so that when a singer entered
the audience would at once guess the kind of character he
or she represented. So Cadmus is dressed as an old king
out of a fairy-tale, thousands of years old, Tiresias as an

Anglican archdeacon, Pentheus like a portrait of one of those pious mediaeval kings, Dionysus as a Regency dandy, Agave and Autonoe in the fashion of the Second Empire, and when, near the end, the chorus of Bassarids swarms on to the stage, they are dressed as Beats.

This has been, I fear, a self-indulgent talk. I hope at least that, despite my self-indulgence or because of it, I have conveyed to you some of my enthusiasm, as a poet, for opera as a form of drama in which the poet may play a role, minor though it be.

Judging by the poetry they have written, all the modern poets whom I admire seem to share my conviction that in this age poetry intended to be spoken or read can no longer be written in a High, even in a golden style, only in a Drab one, to use these terms as Professor C. S. Lewis has used them. By a Drab style I mean a quiet tone of voice which deliberately avoids drawing attention to itself as Poetry with a capital P, and a modesty of gesture. Whenever a modern poet raises his voice, he makes me feel embarrassed, like a man wearing a wig or elevator shoes.

I have – I imagine most of my colleagues have too – my theories about why this should be so, but I shall not bore you by inflicting them on you. For non-dramatic poetry this raises no problem; for verse drama it does. In writing his verse plays Mr Eliot took, I believe, the only possible line. Except at a few unusual moments, he kept the style Drab. I cannot think, however, that he was altogether happy at having to do this, for to perform in public is, as we say, 'to put on an act'; this a High style can unashamedly do, but a Drab style has to pretend it is not 'making a scene'. What I have tried to show you is that, as an art-form involving words, opera is the last refuge of the High style, the only art to which a poet with a nostalgia for those times past, when poets could write in the grand manner all by themselves, can still contribute, provided he will take the pains to learn the *métier* and is lucky enough to find a composer he can believe in.

IV

WORDS AND THE WORD

The Book of Genesis gives two accounts of the creation of Man by God. In Chapter I, vv. 27–8 it is said: 'Male and female created He them, and God said "Be fruitful and multiply".' In Chapter II, v. 7, 'God formed man of the dust of the ground and breathed into his nostrils the breath of life; and man became a living soul'; and the reason given in v. 18 for the creation of Eve is not biological but personal: 'It is not good that the man should be alone.'

Every human being, that is to say, is at one and the same time both an individual member of the biological species, *Homo sapiens*, which came into being by the process of natural selection, and a unique person, with a unique perspective on the world, endowed with a consciousness which is a Trinity-in-Unity. As St Augustine said: 'I am willing and knowing; I know that I am and will; I will to be and to know.' The human condition is further complicated by the fact that man is a history – and culture-making creature, who by his own efforts has been able to change himself after his biological evolution was complete. Each of us, therefore, has acquired what we call a 'second nature', created by the particular society and culture into which we happen to have been born. Here the distinction between individual and person becomes blurred. To use the term individual not only as a biological description – a man, a woman, a child, a blonde, etc., but also as a social, cultural one – an Englishman, a Frenchman, a German – is correct to the degree that our thoughts and

103

behaviour, however personal we may imagine them to be, are seen by an outsider to be the result of social conditioning. The society to which we belong, may, on the other hand, be legitimately termed a corporate person.

As individuals, then, we are created by sexual reproduction and social conditioning and are what we are, not by our free choice but by the accident of birth and economic necessity. As individuals we do not act; we exhibit behaviour characteristic of the biological species and social group or groups to which we belong. As individuals we are countable, comparable, replaceable.

As persons who can, now and again, truthfully say *I*, we are called into being – the myth of our common descent from a single ancestor, Adam, is a way of saying this – not by any biological process but by other persons, our parents, our siblings, our friends. As persons we are not willy-nilly members of a society but are free to form communities, groups of rational beings, united, as St Augustine said, by a love of something other than themselves – God, music, stamp-collecting or what-have-you. As persons we are capable of deeds, of choosing to do this rather than that and accepting responsibility for the consequences whatever they may turn out to be. As persons we are uncountable, incomparable, irreplaceable.

Any consideration of the nature of language must begin with distinguishing between our use of words as a code of communication between individuals and our use of them for personal speech. Many animals have a code of communication, auditory or visual or olfactory signals by which individual members of the species convey to each other information about food, sex, territory, the presence of enemies, etc., which is essential to their survival; and in social animals like the bee, this code may become extremely complex. But no animal, so far as we know, addresses another personally, though some domesticated animals like dogs can respond to their names when addressed by humans. All animal signals, one might say, are statements

in the third person. Our use of words as a code is best
illustrated by a phrase book for tourists, giving the equivalent in other languages for such remarks as 'Can you tell
me the way to the station?' If I ask this question, I do not
ask it out of idle curiosity but because it is essential to me
to know the answer if I am to catch my train. The individual
of whom I ask it has no personal interest for me, nor I for
him. Once I have asked and he has answered we cease to
exist for each other. So far as both of us are concerned, we
might be two other people. It so happens that in English it
is the grammatical convention to use the second person
'you' and the first person 'me' in such a sentence, but this
is a pure convention. The third person would do equally
well, and some languages use it in such circumstances. In
Italian, for example, when addressing people with whom
one is not on intimate terms, one uses the third person *lei*.

When speaking in my own linguistic code, I know in
advance exactly what I am going to say: the words are in
no sense 'mine'. And, provided that the way of life and
social needs of two linguistic groups are the same, exact
translation from one language into the other is possible.
Provided a culture has a railway, it will have a word
meaning 'station'. If we only used words as a communication code, then it seems probable that, as with animals,
the human species would only have one language with, at
most, dialect variations like the song of the chaffinch.

But as persons we are capable of speech proper. In
speech one unique person addresses another unique person
and does so voluntarily: he could keep silent if he chose.
We speak as persons because we desire to disclose ourselves to each other and to share our experiences, not
because we need to share them, but because we enjoy
sharing them. When we genuinely speak, we do not have
the words ready to do our bidding; we have to find them,
and we do not know exactly what we are going to say until
we have said it, and we say and hear something new that
has never been said or heard before. Here are three

statements about speech which deserve to be remembered. The first is by Karl Kraus:

> Speech is the mother, not the handmaid, of thought.

The second is by Lichtenberg:

> I have drawn from the well of language many a thought which I did not have and could not put into words.

The last is by Rosenstock-Huessy:

> Living language always overpowers the thinking of the individual man. It is wiser than the thinker who assumes that he thinks whereas he only speaks and in so doing faithfully trusts the material of language; it guides his concepts unconsciously towards an unknown future.

To understand the nature of speech, we must begin not with statements in the third person, like 'The cat is on the mat', but with proper names, the first and second personal pronouns and words of summons and command, response and obedience: 'Adam, where art thou? Lord, here am I. Follow me. Be it unto me according to thy word.'

Parents give each child a name. Among primitive tribes these names are more often tecnonyms, defining the child's relationship to living kindred, or necronyms, defining his relationship to the dead, than autonyms. But whatever system of naming is used, the effect on the child is the same. Hearing himself called by his name, he becomes aware of himself as a unique person. As uttered by his parents, his name is prenominally the second person singular 'thou'. In responding, his name is prenominally the first person singular *I*. The second person precedes the first; we respond and obey before we can summon and command. In modern societies we have family names, defining our relation both to the dead and to the living, and first names which are autonyms, belonging within our generation and family to ourselves alone.

Two children in the same family are never given the same name.

Among Christians it is customary to name a child after a saint. The saint has no biological relationship to the child: he is not an ancestor. In so naming him, the parents declare that this child is not only their child, an extension of themselves, but also a child of God, a new creation.

Throughout life our existence is profoundly influenced by names – names of persons we meet and love, names of characters, whether in history or fiction, who embody for us what we mean by goodness, justice, courage, names of artists and scientists who have helped to form our conception of life and the world. Indeed, one might say: 'Give me a list of the names in your life, and I will tell you who you are.'

Nor is it only the names of human beings that are important to us. It is our right and duty, as it was Adam's, to give names to all things, and to any thing or creature which arouses our affection we desire to give a proper name. Even in the case of generic names only flowers and animals which we can name are quite real to us. As Thoreau said: 'With a knowledge of the name comes a distincter recognition and knowledge of things.'

Because they designate unique beings, proper names are untranslatable. When translating a German novel, the hero of which is named Heinrich, the translator will leave the name as it is; he will not anglicize it to Henry.

The name of a human being designates him or her both as an individual and as a person; for this reason the name has male or female gender. But the first and second personal pronouns, which we use when addressing each other as persons, have no gender. The third personal pronoun has gender and is therefore, strictly speaking, impersonal. It is grammatically convenient when speaking of someone who is not present to say 'he' or 'she', but if, when we do so, we think of them as 'he' or 'she', not as

John or Sheila, then we are thinking of them, not as persons but as individuals.*

Whenever we use the pronouns 'you' and 'I', not as a mere convention, but meaning what we say, uttering them is accompanied by a characteristic feeling-tone.

The you-feeling is a feeling of attributing-responsibility-to. If a boy says to a girl, 'You are beautiful', and means what he says, he is asserting that she is, in part at least, responsible for her physical appearance: it is not merely the result of a lucky combination of genes. If a man says to someone who has done him an injury 'I forgive you,' he is asserting that the other is not a lunatic or a thing but a person who knew what he was doing and to whom.

Similarly, the I-feeling is one of accepting-responsibility-for. To say 'I love you' is to say that, whatever the causes or the origin of what I feel, I take upon myself the responsibility for them; I am not the passive and helpless victim of passion. Common to both the I- and the You-feeling is the feeling of being in the middle of a story with a personal past to remember and a personal future to make.

As I said earlier, it is characteristic of code statements that equivalents exist in all languages. Failure in communication may occur through simple ignorance and

---

* Whether Dr Bruno Bettleheim's theory that the cause of autism in children is a conviction that their parents wish they did not exist is correct or not, I am in no position to judge. But the linguistic behaviour of autistic children, as recorded in his book, *The Empty Fortress*, is of great interest.

One such child, 'Joey', who had earlier given up using the personal pronouns altogether, began, after some treatment, to use them again, but in reverse. He referred to himself as 'you' and to the adult he was speaking to as 'I'. After further treatment he was able to use 'I' correctly and to name some of the children in addition to his therapist. But he never used proper names or personal pronouns in direct address, only in the indirect third person when referring to them. He never referred to anyone by name; others were simply *that person:* later, with some differentiation, 'the small person' or 'the big person'.

misunderstanding. Trying to ask in German the way to the station, I may say *Hof* meaning 'farm' instead of *Bahnhof*. And if I am in a big city, it is possible that the individual I ask gives me wrong directions. But since we are strangers, with no personal interest in each other, I can usually assume that his answer is meant to be true: I exclude the possibility of a deliberate lie because I cannot imagine his having a motive for deceiving me.

Personal speech presents much more difficult problems. Even when two persons share the same mother-tongue, they do not speak it in exactly the same way: what the speaker says in the light of his experience, the listener has to interpret in the light of his, and these are not the same. Every dialogue is a feat of translation. As Rosenzweig said:

To translate means to serve two masters – something nobody can do. Hence, as is true of all things that in theory no one can do – it becomes in practice everybody's job. Everyone must translate and everyone does translate. Whoever speaks is translating his thought for the comprehension he expects from the other, not from a 'general' other but from this particular other in front of him, whose eyes widen with eagerness or close with boredom. The listener translates the words which reach his ears into the language he himself uses. The theoretical impossibility of translation can mean to us only that in the course of the 'impossible' – necessary compromises which in their sequence make the stuff of life – this theoretical impossibility will give us the courage of a modesty which will then demand of the translation not anything impossible but simply what must be done. Thus, in speaking of listening, the 'other' need not have my ears or my mouth – which would render unnecessary not only translation but also speaking and listening. What is needed is neither a translation that is so far from being a translation as to be the original – this would eliminate the listener – nor one that is in effect a new original – this would eliminate the speaker.

In the case of code statements not only can I assume that I am not being lied to but also that if a failure of communication occurs, it will soon be made manifest: either I get to the station or I don't. But when we speak as persons self-interest, malice, etc., often make us tell deliberate lies, and in most cases the lie cannot be empirically proved or disproved. If a boy says to a girl, 'I love you', she must either believe it, doubt it or deny it. 'Belief, doubt, denial', as Pascal said, 'are to human beings what the race is to the horse.' We must, however, believe before we can learn to doubt and deny. Deprived of the guidance of inborn instincts, the human species has to walk by faith. If a child were to begin by doubting everything its parents said to it, it would never learn to talk. To lie, even with the best of intentions, is a deadly sin, for every time we tell someone a lie, even with the best intentions, we not only forfeit for ever the right to his faith in us, we undermine his faith in all men and all speech. It is with good reason that the devil is called the father of lies.

Scepticism, said Santayana, is the chastity of the intellect. Precisely. But a chastity which is not founded upon a deep reverence for sex is nothing but tight-arsed old-maidery.

There are other misuses of language which, in the long run, probably do more damage than the deliberate lie. He who tells a deliberate lie is aware of what he is doing; lying may corrupt his heart but not his intellect or the language in which he lies. But we corrupt our hearts, our intellects and our language when we use words for purposes to which the judgement 'true' or 'false' is irrelevant.

We can, for instance, speak not because we have anything we believe is important to say but because we are afraid of silence or of not being noticed. And we can listen to or read the words of others not in order to learn something but because we are bored and need to fill up our time. Cocktail-party chatter and journalism in the pejorative sense are two aspects of the same disease, what the Bible calls idle words for which at Judgement Day God will hold us accountable. Since the chatterer has nothing he really wishes to say and the journalist nothing he really wishes to write, it is of no consequence to either what words they actually use. Hence it is not long before the exact meanings of words and their precise grammatical relations are forgotten, and presently, without knowing it, they are talking and writing nonsense.

This kind of corruption of language has been enormously encouraged by mass education and the mass media. Until quite recently most people spoke the language of the social class to which they belonged. Their vocabulary might be limited, but they had learned it at first-hand from their parents and neighbours, so that they knew the correct meaning of such words as they did use and made no attempt to use any others. Today I would guess that nine-tenths of the population do not know what 30 per cent of the words they use actually mean. Thus, it is possible to hear someone who is feeling sick say, 'I am nauseous', for a reviewer of a spy-thriller to describe it as 'enervating' and for a television star to say of an investment agency which was sponsoring his programme, 'They are integrity-ridden.'

To make polite conversation is, of course, essential to a civilized society, and if idleness of speech has become such a problem in our time, one of the reasons is that polite conversation is no longer regarded as an art which has to be learned. When we are children the only society we know is a society of intimates, parents, nurses, brothers and sisters. It is only as we grow up that we encounter strangers, some of whom may in the future become intimate friends, others casual acquaintances, while others we shall never see again, and we have to learn that we cannot speak to strangers or, for that matter, to the public in the same way that we speak to intimates. One of the worst characteristics of present-day society is its childish indiscretion, which ignores this difference. Both in conversation and in books people today are only too ready to take their clothes off in front of total strangers.

Again, while it is a great blessing that a man no longer has to be rich in order to enjoy the masterpieces of the past, for paperbacks, first-rate colour reproductions and stereo-phonograph records have made them available to all but the very poor, this ease of access, if misused – and we do misuse it – can become a curse. We are all of us tempted to read more books, look at more pictures, listen to more music than we can possibly absorb, and the result of such gluttony is not a cultured mind but a consuming one; what it reads, looks at, listens to is immediately forgotten, leaving no more traces behind it than yesterday's newspaper.

More deadly still is the use of words as 'black magic'. Like the 'white magic' of poetry, 'black magic' is concerned with enchantment. But while the poet is himself enchanted by the subjects he writes about and wishes only to share his enchantment with others, the black magician is perfectly cold. He has no enchantment to share with others but uses enchantment as a way of securing domination over others and compelling them to do his will. He does not ask for a free response to his spell; he demands a tautological echo.

In all ages the technique of the black magician has been essentially the same. In all spells the words are deprived of their meanings and reduced to syllables or verbal noises. This may be done literally, as when magicians used to recite the Lord's Prayer backwards, or by reiterating a word over and over again as loudly as possible until it has become a mere sound. For millions of people today words like communism, capitalism, imperialism, peace, freedom, democracy have ceased to be words, the meaning of which can be inquired into and discussed, and have become right or wrong noises to which the response is as involuntary as a knee reflex.

It makes no difference if the magic is being employed

simply for the aggrandizement of the magician himself or if, as is more usual, he claims to be serving some good cause. Indeed, the better the cause he claims to be serving, the more evil he does. Most commercial advertising, revoltingly vulgar though it be, is comparatively harmless. If advertising conditions me to buy a certain brand of toilet soap, provided that the law prevents the sale of a substance that poisons my skin or leaves me dirtier than I was before, it makes no difference to my body or my soul which brand I use. Political and religious propaganda are another matter, for politics and religion are spheres where personal choice is essential. 'God,' said St Augustine, 'who made us without our help, will not save us without our consent.' Propaganda, like the sword, attempts to eliminate consent or dissent, and in our age magical language has to a great extent replaced the sword.

I can imagine – though I know, thank God, that it will never happen – the following situation. A group of pious multi-millionaires buy time on radio and TV at a moment when the Church happens to have at its disposal a number of brilliant demagogic evangelists, who know all the tricks of appeal. Bombarded by sermons, religious movies and musicals, the public is persuaded that to go to church is to be 'with it', so that presently all the churches are full every Sunday. What would this signify? Neither more nor less than the forcible mass conversions of the barbarians in the eighth and ninth centuries.

This, at least, can be said for poetry. It cannot be employed by the black magician; if one responds to a poem at all, the response is conscious and voluntary. And it cannot, it would seem, be reduced to an idle word. Novels, even good ones, can be idly read simply to pass the time; music, even the greatest, can be treated as background noise. But nobody has yet learned to consume a poem. If one can take it at all, then one can only listen to it as its author intended it to be listened to.

Poetry is personal speech in its purest form. It is

concerned, and only concerned, with human beings as unique persons. What men do from necessity or by second nature as individual members of a society cannot be the subject of poetry, for poetry is gratuitous utterance. As Paul Valéry said: 'In poetry everything that must be said cannot be said well.' It is essentially a spoken, not a written, word. One can never grasp a poem one is reading unless one hears the actual sound of the words, and its meaning is the outcome of a dialogue between the words of the poem and the response of whoever is listening to them. Not only is every poem unique, but its significance is unique for each person who responds to it. In so far as one can speak of poetry as conveying knowledge, it is the kind of knowledge implied by the biblical phrase 'Then Adam knew Eve his wife'; knowing is inseparable from being known. To say that poetry is ultimately concerned only with human persons does not, of course, mean that it is always overtly about them. We are always intimately related to non-human natures, and unless we try to understand and relate to what we are not, we shall never understand what we are. The poet has to preserve and express by art what primitive peoples knew instinctively, namely, that for man nature is a realm of sacramental analogies. As Emerson wrote:

> Man is an analogist and studies relations in all objects. He is placed in the centre of beings and a ray of relation passes from every being to him. And neither can man be understood without these objects, nor these objects without man. All the facts in natural history taken by themselves have no value, but are barren like a single sex. But marry it to human history and it is full of life. Because of this radical correspondence between visible things and human thoughts, in poetry all spiritual facts are represented by natural symbols.

To say that a poem is a personal utterance does not mean that it is an act of self-expression. The experience a poet endeavours to embody in a poem is an experience of a reality common to all men; it is only his in that this reality is perceived from a perspective which nobody but he can occupy.

What by providence he has been the first to perceive it is his duty to share with others. A theological explanation of this has been given by George MacDonald:

> In every man there is an inner chamber of peculiar life into which God only may enter. There is also a chamber in God himself into which none can enter but the one, the peculiar man – out of which chamber that man has to bring revelation and strength to his brethren. That is that for which he was made – to reveal the secret things of the Father.

Again, though a poet speaks as a person, he is not a disembodied angel but an individual member of the human species, born at a particular time in a particular place. Unique though it be, every genuine work of art exhibits two qualities, Permanence and Nowness. By Permanence I mean that it continues to be relevant to human experience long after its maker and the society to which he belonged have passed away. By Nowness I mean those characteristics of language, style, presuppositions about the nature of the universe and of man, etc., which enable an art historian to give at least an approximate date for its making.

The job of the arts is to manifest the personal and the chosen: the study of the impersonal and the necessary is the job of the sciences. Though the object of its concern is necessity, science is just as gratuitous and personal a human activity as art. To suppose that the sciences can tell us what things are really like, independent of our minds, is a myth. Scientific knowledge, however, is not reciprocal, like artistic knowledge, but one-way; what the scientist knows cannot know him. For scientific purposes, therefore, words, however abstract, are too personal to be an adequate language. Science could not realize its true nature until it had invented an impersonal universal

115

language from which every vestige of poetry has been eliminated, namely algebra, of which Whitehead says:

> Algebra reverses the relative importance of the factors in ordinary language. It is essentially a written language, and it endeavours to exemplify in its written structure the patterns which it is its purpose to convey. The pattern of the marks on paper is a particular instance of the pattern to be conveyed to thought. The algebraic method is the best approach to the expression of necessity by reason of its reduction of accident to the ghost-like character of the real variable.

Both the Old and New Testament define the activities of God as Creator and His relations to men in terms of human speech.

> God said: Let there be light.

> For as the rain cometh down and the snow from heaven, and returneth not thither, but watereth the earth and maketh it bring forth and bud, that it may give seed to the earth, so shall my word be that goeth forth out of my mouth. It shall not return unto me void, but it shall accomplish that which I please, and it shall prosper in the thing whereto I sent it.

> Man shall not live by bread alone, but by the word that proceedeth out of the mouth of God.

As the use of the singular indicates, such statements are analogical, not literal. As human beings, we speak in sentences made up of a number of words, and we must speak them in a particular language. So speak the gods in the *Iliad*, both to each other and to men. They make speeches, and they make them in Greek. But when the Elohist makes God say to Abraham: 'Take Isaac, thine only son whom thou lovest', we are not to think that Hebrew is the language spoken by God or that Jehovah, like Zeus, has vocal chords which make audible sounds.

What, then, is the analogy intended to assert?

116

First, that God is not an object but a person, not a concept but a name. It denies, that is, that God is the god of Greek philosophy, *To Theon*, who can neither speak nor be spoken to, only contemplated. As Rosenstock-Huessy says: 'To approach God as an object of theoretical discussion is to defeat the quest from the start. Nobody can look at God as an object. He is the power which makes us speak. He puts the words of life into our lips.' Or, as Ferdinand Ebner says: 'To speak of God except in a context of prayer is to take His name in vain.'

Second, the analogy asserts that God acts by exercising authority or power, not force or violence: the creature has a role to play in its creation. If somebody knocks me down, that is an act of force; my falling to the ground is in no sense *my* act. If, on the other hand, somebody commands me to lie down, I can either obey or disobey the order. I may obey it for one of two reasons:

1. out of an irresistible passion of fear at the consequence of disobedience; in that case I am forced to obey, and the act is not mine;
2. because I accept the authority of him who gives the command – I believe that he is wiser than I, and that he wishes me well; in this case, my lying down is *my* act.

Third, if God is the word, then men are forbidden all pagan idolatry of words. The curse of Babel is not the fact that there are many diverse languages – diversity in itself is a good – but the idolization by each linguistic group of its own tongue, the attitude implicit in calling somebody who does not speak Greek a barbarian or in saying, as one Frenchman did: 'The great advantage of the French language is that, in it, the words occur in the order in which one thinks them.' It is significant that when the Word was made flesh it spoke a little-known and little esteemed tongue, Aramaic. There is, that is to say, no sacred tongue: the truth can be told in all. Furthermore,

117

the truth is to be spoken to all men, not reserved as an
esoteric possession for a select few.

Last, if the Word was indeed made flesh, then it is
demanded of men that their words and their lives be in
concord. Only he who is true can speak the truth. Truth is
not ideal or abstract but concrete.

> God does not send a message in place of Himself. He comes
> in person to deliver his message, and, moreover, his message
> is not other than Himself.
> The 'Word' that He sends is an utterance only in the sense
> that it proceeds from Him, but not in the sense that what is
> uttered is other than Himself.
> What He communicates to us would not be Himself unless
> that which is communicated proceeded from Him in Himself.
> Thus the Word of God is not only with God, but the Word
> was God.
> The Christian God is not *both* transcendent and immanent.
> He is a reality other than being Who is present to being, by
> which presence He makes being to be.
>
> Leslie Dewart, *The Future of Belief*

To believe this is to call into question the art of poetry
and all the arts. The artist is a maker, not a man of action.
There may be certain falsities of heart that so corrupt the
imagination as to render it impotent to create, but there is
no comprehensible relation between the moral quality of
a maker's life and the aesthetic value of the works he
makes. On the contrary, every artist knows that the
sources of his art are what Yeats called 'the foul rag-and-
bone shop of the heart', its lusts, its hatreds, its envies,
and that Goethe was speaking for all artists when he
wrote:

Poetic fire sank low in me,
When it was good I sought to see;
But up it flamed, up to the sky,
When it was evil I sought to fly.

When the pagan gods appeared to men, they were immediately recognizable as divine by the awe and wonder they aroused in their mortal beholders, and pre-Christian poets were acclaimed as mouthpieces of the gods because their language was the language of magic enchantment. But Christ refuses to enchant; He demands men's faith.

Since the Word was made flesh, it is impossible to imagine God as speaking in anything but the most sober prose. If Blake was right in saying that Milton was of the Devil's party without knowing it, this is because while it is perfectly credible that Lucifer should speak in a High style, to give God admirable speeches to deliver is to turn him into a Zeus without Zeus' vices. As the German pietist Hamann rightly observed: 'If, when God said "Let there be light", the angels had applauded, wouldn't God have said, "Did I say anything particularly silly?"'

In consequence, the Christian theologian is placed in the difficult position of having to use words, which by their nature are anthropomorphic, to refute anthropomorphic conceptions of God. Yet when such anthropomorphic conceptions are verbally asserted, he must speak: he cannot refute them by silence. Dogmatic theological statements are to be comprehended neither as logical propositions nor as poetic utterances: they are to be taken, rather, as shaggy-dog stories: they have a point, but he who tries too hard to get it will miss it.

The poet, who is concerned not with the Creator but with his creatures, is in a less awkward position, but for him too the relation between words and the truth is problematical. One might say that for Truth the word 'silence' is the least inadequate metaphor, and that words can bear witness to silence only as shadows bear witness to light. Sooner or later every poet discovers the truth of Max Picard's remark: 'The language of the child is silence transformed into sound: the language of the adult is sound that seeks for silence.'

The only witness to the living God, that is to say, which

poetry can bear is indirect and negative. The gods of polytheism were false, but poetry attributed to them one quality which they share with the living God: they were persons who could speak to men and to whom men could respond. Poetry cannot prove the existence of God. It can say only: 'If He exists, He cannot be the abstract God of the philosophers.' The witness of science is complementary. It can say only: 'If God exists, then He cannot be a Zeus without Zeus' vices, who imposes His laws upon men as rulers impose laws upon their subjects.' As Wittgenstein said: 'Ethics must be a condition of the world, like logic.' Whatever heresies they may fall into, by the very nature of their work, an artist cannot become a gnostic Manichee, nor a scientist a Pelagian. As Simone Weil wrote: 'Science alone, and only in its purest rigour, can give a precise content to the notion of providence.'

Man was created by God as a culture-making creature, endowed with imagination and reason and capable of artistic fabrication and scientific investigation, so that to say that Christ calls art into question does not mean that it is forbidden to a Christian as it is forbidden to a Platonist, only that the nature of the imagination and the function of the artist are seen otherwise than they were in pre-Christian times. In a magico-polytheistic culture all events are believed to be caused by personal powers who can be understood and to some extent controlled by speech, and the nearest that men can come to the concept of necessity is in the myth of the Fates who determine events by whim; in such a culture, therefore, poets are the theologians, the sacred mouthpieces of society; it is they who teach the myths and rescue from oblivion the great deeds of ancestral heroes. That to which the imagination by its nature responds with excitement, namely, the manifestly extraordinary and powerful, is identified with the divine. The poet is one whose words are equal to his divine subjects, which can happen only if he is divinely inspired. The coming of Christ in the form of a servant who cannot be recognized by the eye of flesh and blood, only by the eye of faith, puts an end to all such claims. The imagination is to be regarded as a natural faculty, the subject matter of which is the phenomenal world, not its Creator. For a poet brought up in a Christian society it is perfectly possible to write a poem on a Christian theme, but when he does so he is concerned with it as an aspect of a religion – that is to say, a human cultural fact, like other facts – not as a matter of faith. The poet is not there to convert the world.

The contrast between the claim of the Gospel narratives to be the Word of God, and the outward appearance and social status of the characters in them must, if the claim is believed, abolish the assumptions of the classical aesthetic, as Professor Auerbach has demonstrated in his remarkable book, *Mimesis*. Speaking of the account of Peter's denial, he says:

> Both the nature and scene of the conflict also fall entirely outside the domain of classical antiquity. Viewed superficially the thing is a police action and its consequences; it takes place entirely among everyday men and women of the common people; anything of the sort could be thought of in antique terms only as farce or comedy. A scene like Peter's denial fits into no antique genre. It is too serious for comedy, too contemporary and everyday for tragedy, politically too insignificant for history, and the form which was given it is one of such immediacy that its like does not exist in the literature of antiquity. This can be judged by a symptom which at first glance may seem insignificant – the use of direct discourse. Direct discourse is generally restricted in the antique historians to great continuous speeches delivered to the senate or before a popular assembly, but here in the scene of Peter's denial – the dramatic tension of the moment when the actors stand face to face has been given an immediacy compared with which the stichomactry of antique tragedy appears highly stylized.

The Gospels shattered the classical conventions, but it

would be wrong to suppose that they replaced them by any positive aesthetic principles. They made and make it possible for artists to look for subjects in areas which they had hitherto ignored, but the nature of the human imagination, as of the human reason, cannot change. It is excited only by what seems to it extraordinary, and it can deal only with what it can make publicly interesting. For example, neither in poetry nor fiction is there, I believe, a convincing portrait of a saint. Sanctity, it would seem, can be hinted at only by comic indirection, as in *Don Quixote*.

One event described in the New Testament has, in the long run, had a great cultural influence, namely, Pentecost. The gift of the Holy Spirit on that occasion is generally called the gift of tongues. It might more aptly be called the gift of ears. I have never been able to understand how belly-talkers, from Montanus to the Irvingites, can have taken the story in Acts to mean that to make verbal noises which nobody else could understand was a proof of divine inspiration. What happened at Pentecost was exactly the opposite, a miracle of instantaneous translation: 'Behold are not all these which speak Galileans. And now hear we every man in his own tongue wherein we were born, hear them speak in our own tongue the wonderful works of God.' The curse of Babel, one might say, was redeemed because, for the first time, men were willing, in absolute fullness of heart, to speak and to listen not merely to their sort of person but to total strangers.

The immediate result of Pentecost, when the Church was summoned to convert the world, was that the Scriptures had to be translated into other languages. Translation had been relatively rare in the classical world; most educated persons knew both Latin and Greek and were incurious about what was written in any other tongue. When the Empire collapsed the translation of the Scriptures into barbarian tongues was followed in time by the translation of literary and philosophical works, so that today there is no literature produced by one linguistic group which has not been profoundly influenced by that of another. Anybody who loves language knows that he cannot fully understand his mother-tongue without a working knowledge of at least two other languages, just as one cannot understand one's mother country without having lived in at least two others.

Language, as such, is the concern of every human being at all times, but artists whose medium is language, that is to say, poets and novelists, have special problems of their own, and these vary with times and places. In certain cultures, polytheistic societies, for example, and in certain historical epochs, like the Romantic age, literary artists have been accorded a public status which has tempted them to think of themselves more highly than they ought to think. Today they are in danger of not taking their art seriously enough. Their reaction to their diminished status may take two forms. They may, in a futile attempt to recover social importance, attempt to become propagandists for some good cause – to be, as current jargon has it, *engagé*. The world about us is, as it always has been, full of gross evils and appalling misery, but it is a fatal delusion and a shocking overestimation of the importance of the artist in the world to suppose that by making works of art we can do anything to eradicate the one or alleviate the other. The political and social history of Europe would be what it has been if Dante, Shakespeare, Goethe, Titian, Mozart, Beethoven *et al.* had never existed. Where social evils are concerned the only effective weapons are two: political action and straight reportage of the facts – journalism in the good sense. Art is impotent.* The utmost

---

* An artist can become a figure of political importance if, and only if, he is personally persecuted by the authorities, temporal or spiritual. Under dogmatic and authoritarian governments which can control all sources of public information (societies, that is to say, in which honest journalism does not exist) a poet or a novelist can on occasion say something which escapes the censor's eye and has real political impact because the public cannot hear the truth from any other source, and the fact that he is risking his personal safety to say it gives him moral authority.

an artist can hope to do for his contemporary readers is, as
Dr Johnson said, to enable them a little better to enjoy life
or a little better to endure it. Further, let us remember
that though the great artists of the past could not change
the course of history, it is only through their work that we
are able to break bread with the dead, and without communion with the dead a fully human life is impossible.

The opposite reaction is to imagine that if it is true, and
I think it is, that art cannot be effective as serious action,
then let it be frivolous action: instead of making political
speeches, let us invent happenings. But the pop artist,
like his *engagé* brother, forgets that the artist is not a
man of action but a maker, a fabricator of objects. To
believe in the value of art is to believe that it is possible to
make an object, be it an epic or a two-line epigram, which
will remain permanently on hand in the world. The prob-
abilities of success are against him, but an artist must not
attempt anything less. Until quite recently this seemed
self-evident, for all fabrication was carried on in the same
way. Houses, furniture, tools, linens, tableware, wedding
dresses, etc., were made to last and be handed on from one
generation to the next. This is no longer the case: such
things are now deliberately designed to become obsolete
in a few years. This, however deplorable, is possible because
such craft objects are to some extent necessary: men must
have dwelling-places, chairs and so on. But the so-called
'fine' arts which are purely gratuitous – nobody has to
write or read a poem or a novel – cannot follow this path
without becoming extinct.

In defending us against losing our nerve, let us take
comfort from the masterpieces of the past, for one thing
they have to teach us is that social and technological
change are not as fatal to a genuine work of art as we are
inclined to fear. Our world is already utterly different
from the worlds in which they were created, yet we can
still comprehend and enjoy them.

The future indeed looks gloomy, but the change in our

ways of thought seems to me encouraging. Since the end of the eighteenth century until quite recently, the scientists believed – and succeeded in convincing most people they were right – that, to quote C. S. Lewis, 'by inferences from our sense-experience (improved by instruments) we could know the ultimate physical reality more or less as, by maps, pictures and travel books, a man can know a country he has not visited; and that in both cases the truth would be a sort of mental replica of the thing itself'. A good many of them went even further and claimed that it would be found in the end that all mental events could be reduced to physical events and known in this manner. Consequently, our forbears were haunted by the fear that scientific discoveries might be made which would abolish all traditional beliefs and wisdom. From Copernicus to Darwin to Freud every important discovery created a hullabaloo. The conservatives refused to believe that there could be any truth in them, and the radicals drew theological and philosophical conclusions which the discoveries in themselves did not warrant. Among artists there were two reactions: some tried to become as much like scientists as possible and banded together under the slogan 'naturalism'; others averted their eyes from the phenomenal world altogether, as the abode of Satan, and tried to create purely aesthetic worlds out of their subjective feelings.

Now, however, there is no reason why anyone should be either a doctrinaire naturalist or a doctrinaire aesthete, for the scientists have discovered that objective knowledge of things-in-themselves is not attainable. As Werner Heisenberg has said:

When we speak of the picture of nature in the exact science of our age, we do not mean a picture of nature so much as a picture of our relationships with nature. Science no longer confronts nature as an objective observer, but sees himself as an actor in this interplay between man and nature. The

125

scientific method of analysing, explaining and classifying has become conscious of its limitations, which arise out of the fact that by its intervention science alters and refashions the object of its investigation. In other words, method and object can no longer be separated. The scientific world view has ceased to be a scientific view in the true sense of the word.

How utterly bewildered and shocked a nineteenth-century physicist would have been, had he been able to attend a meeting at which Wolfgang Pauli read a paper. In the discussion which followed Neils Bohr said: 'We are all agreed your theory is crazy. What divides us is whether it is crazy enough to stand a chance of being correct. My own opinion is that it is not crazy enough.'

We seem to have reached a point where if the word 'real' can be used at all, then the only world which is 'real' for us, as in the world in which all of us, including scientists, are born, work, love, hate and die, is the primary phenomenal world as it is and always has been presented to us through our senses, a world in which the sun moves across the sky from east to west, the stars are hung like lamps in the vault of heaven, the measure of magnitude is the human body and objects are either in motion or at rest.

If this be accepted, it is possible that artists may become both more modest and more self-assured, that they may develop both a sense of humour about their vocation and a respect for that most admirable of Roman deities, the god Terminus. No poet will then produce the kind of work which demands that a reader spend his whole life reading it and nothing else. The claim to be a 'genius' will become as strange as it would have seemed to the Middle Ages. There might even be a return, in a more sophisticated form, to a belief in the phenomenal world as a realm of sacred analogies.

But this is guessing. In the meantime, and whatever is going to happen, we must carry on as best as we can. I am certain that I am speaking for many others as well as myself when I say what comfort, in hours of doubt and discouragement, I have derived from thinking of the example set, both as a poet and as a human being, by the man in whose memory these lectures have been founded.